SOLVING THE SPIRITUAL DILEMMA

Solving The Spiritual Dilemma

Why is Discernment the Key to Receiving Eternal Life?

MICHAEL COPPLE

E G Publishing

First Printing, 2022

Dedicated to

James Dean Steele
11 January 1944 – 15 September 2021

Just three months prior to the Lord taking him home, Jim Steele edited this book with great attention to detail. I will forever be grateful for his knowledge and caring attitude. Valedictorian of His 1962 class of Webb City, Missouri High School, and five decades later, WCHS Hall of Fame inductee, he was a life-long friend who I was honored to stand beside when we received our Eagle Scout awards. I am thankful for his loving support in my every endeavor throughout our entire lives. I genuinely, deeply appreciate his service to our nation, as he was a US Air Force Captain and Vietnam veteran who served near the DMZ for one full year. Most of all, I am sincerely looking forward to seeing Jim Steele again, because he is a fellow born-again believer in the Lord Jesus Christ our God and Savior.

Acknowledgments

First, I give deepest, sincere gratitude to our Triune God for the life changing relationship He has given me with the Lord Jesus Christ. This new life and hope have motivated me to hunger more and more for His truth and to spread His love with God's Word.

God took Randy Amos home on the night of 3 to 4 November 2020. Our brother is face to face with the Lord Jesus Christ, and I believe he is hearing those words from the Savior: *"Well done, good and faithful servant."* The gift of teaching which the Holy Spirit bestowed upon our brother Randy is still reaping fruit and will continue for the rest of time. I pray that the Lord would let him know my heartfelt gratefulness.

I'd like to offer special thanks to Jabe Nicholson, not only for the edification he transmits in our regular listening to the *Uplook Ministries* messages, but also for the inspiration of restored automobile photos in chapter three. Since he and six young men came through Golden, B.C., Canada with the 50's model refurbished cars and evangelic truths, I haven't stopped thinking about it. The young men with Jabe were Josh Caplan, Stephen Dick, Jayson Ball, Dale Martin, Elijah Middleton, and Keith Trevolt. I am deeply thankful for how they all roused the thought of comparing a restored car to that of a ruined but renewed soul.

I extend my gratitude to our brother and sister in Christ, Theo Wiersma, who is now at home with the Lord, and his widow, Donna Wiersma. Theo skillfully "rescued" the ruined car from the pasture with his tractor and carefully loaded it onto the trailer. I appreciate Donna kindly granting permission to use the photos.

Jim Steele, life-long friend and dear brother in Christ, spent what I believe had to be many painstaking hours meticulously editing the manuscript for *Solving the Spiritual Dilemma*. I will forever be sincerely appreciative for his attention to detail, manner of modest corrections (to prevent me from being too embarrassed), and yet, thoroughness for a professional end product. He wrote this statement in his return of the many pages of manuscript: "Thank you for sending it, that I might find some light in our dark, increasingly foreboding world."

Brother in Christ, US Air Force veteran, F-15 pilot, and Academy Wings of Blue Parachute Team member, Al Wallace read yet another of our manuscripts and provided the following feedback for which I am deeply humbled and very grateful: "You have set a new standard for providing Biblical and other references for your assertions — quite impressive."

Peter Kerr, author of *Election and Predestination*, long-time teacher at Kawartha Lakes Bible College, Peterborough, ON, and present Canadian Director of the Emmaus Correspondence School, overwhelmed me by "focusing on the content" with the following positive review: "I thoroughly enjoyed the book, and appreciate the solid Scriptural authority throughout. I realize the material is counter-cultural and not politically correct, but the truth is so needed in these times. I pray the

Lord creates the opening for publishing and to get it into the hands of teachable souls."

Other solid, gifted brothers in the Lord Jesus Christ who've helped me grow in my walk with the Lord are Warren Henderson, Louis Voyer, Ed Anthony, Harold Summers, Mike Atwood, Steve Price, and more. I am extremely grateful to these brothers who've devoted so much of their lives to the Lord and have helped us understand God's absolute truth and to better know Him and love Him by writing books and commentaries, and speaking on "Zoom" and at conferences. Most have even come to the little assembly meeting of the Columbia Valley Bible Fellowship at Parson, BC to bring messages that encourage the saints with growing knowledge of our Lord God and Savior.

I continue to thank my brother in Christ and mentor, Ralph Kirchhofer, who has further developed my walk with the Lord *moment by moment* for the past 16 years. He has often boosted my confidence and reminded and instilled in me that *in all things the Lord Jesus Christ may have the preeminence.*

I will never stop thanking my loving, equally yoked wife, Elfriede Copple, who has a fulltime job editing, marketing, and communicating with publishers' staffs. Elfriede's gifts of administration and longsuffering were incalculable for supporting me to make this book public. I give her my heartfelt, deep appreciation. She and I both hope this book will make a positive impact for the Lord's purpose. To God be the glory.

I thank my dad and mom for instilling a foundation of patriotism, moral values and faith; and for the way they raised my brother and sisters and myself with unfailing love and energy. I would not be the person I am today without what they have done for me.

Introduction

All Scripture quotations are from the King James Version (KJV) of the Bible unless otherwise noted.

Within the Scriptures there are sometimes [brackets] with explanations of the meaning of older, out of date English words not commonly used today. Those bracketed, up-to-date words are either taken from the Bible margins, or from the author, to provide ease of understanding or clarification.

To make sense in English, the KJV Bible *italicized* some added words—words which were not in the original Hebrew, Aramaic, or Greek languages. The following verse demonstrates an example with the word *is*:

All Scripture *is* given by inspiration of God. 2 Timothy 3:16a

The verbs *is* and *are* often were added, but not in every case:

The mystery of God, and of the Father, and of Christ;
in whom are hid all the treasures of wisdom and knowledge.
Colossians 2:2b-3

Contents

Chapter 1

What is Discernment

It is the author's resolute, unshakable belief that time never ends and that eternal continuance of life even outside the physical body is inevitable. Each and every believer has experienced a life-changing relationship with our Savior, Jesus Christ and our Creator. He has been in existence for all eternity. Each and every believer is convinced to have faith in the Triune God—Father, Son, and Holy Spirit. All believers are connected together by believing that the shed blood of Christ is what has forgiven them for offending God. Believers read and come to realize the Bible is absolutely flawless. Every word is the Word of God. The Holy Spirit of God (our Savior), who inspired the writers of the Bible, resides in (indwells) the being of every believer and provides convincing proof (although our physical bodies will die) to one's self that spiritual life is unending. He even adds that we will eventually have new physical, pain free bodies. The following verse, when kept in context with preceding and subsequent verses is referring to the Lord Jesus Christ:

All things were made by him; and without him was not anything made that was made. John 1:3

[20b]the Savior, the Lord Jesus Christ: [21]Who shall change our vile body, that it may be fashioned like unto his glorious body, according to the working whereby he is able even to subdue all things to himself.
Philippians 3:20b-21

Therefore I [Paul the apostle] endure all things for the elect's [those who have made the choice to accept Jesus as their Savior] sake, that they may also obtain the salvation which is in Christ Jesus with eternal glory.
2 Timothy 2:10

A passage in Matthew begins with a man asking Jesus what he must do to have eternal life:
> "What good thing shall I do, that I may have eternal life?" Matthew 19:16b

The passage ends ten verses later with the Lord Jesus saying:
> "With men this is impossible; but with God all things are possible." Matthew 19:26

God makes it possible for each of us to be His children who in turn have eternal life:
> to them gave he [God gave to those who would believe] power [the right] to become the sons [children] of God, *even* to them that believe on his name. John 1:12b

Noah Webster describes *belief*:
> "1. A persuasion of the truth, or [the mind agreeing] to the truth of a declaration" ... "or alleged fact, on the

ground of evidence." ... "2. In theology, faith, or a firm persuasion of the truths of religion."[1]

Making the Wisest Choices Using Discernment

In the 1940's and 1950's, many young kids were fascinated with stories like *The Wizard of Oz*, *Goldilocks and The Three Bears*, *The Three Little Pigs*, and many more. They enjoyed the cartoons: *Bugs Bunny*, *Porky Pig*, *Sylvester the Cat*, and *Elmer Fudd*. They laughed at *The Three Stooges*, *The Keystone Cops, and The Little Rascals*; and after that—back when comedy drove people to laugh without having to use vulgarity—*Red Skelton*, *Jack Benny*, and *Bob Hope* could always make them giggle. Lots of these children wholeheartedly believed in *Super Man* and *Santa Claus*.

They believed the fairy tales that were so intimately instilled within them were sure enough true. But when they grew to be teens, they began to have serious doubts. When those who attended Sunday School attempted to hear the teacher, they couldn't pronounce most of the biblical names of people and places that were being read to them and the other kids; much less understand what was being taught.

When they became adults, they saw the government beginning to tolerate Hollywood movie makers implanting foul language into their productions. This encouraged the comedians to use the same shock techniques to lure audiences—and what had crept in slowly finally erupted into breaking the third Commandment; the use of God's name in vain, to be the norm.

What most Sunday School teaching boiled down to, was educating children to know right from wrong—recognize the difference between honesty and deceitfulness—and know what is *true* and what is *false*.

What does all this have to do with developing discernment? When looking back over those sixty to seventy years of our nation's decline in good values—the degeneracy of the United States—we should consider what our Creator's Word has to say:

> Righteousness exalteth [gives dignity to] a nation: but sin *is* a reproach [shame or disgrace] to any people. Proverbs 14:34

The objective of *Solving the Spiritual Dilemma* is to emphasize the *eternal* impact that discernment can have upon all thoughts, decisions, actions, and reactions in one's very life and being. Furthermore, the purpose is to develop a hunger for the Book that informs how a ruined soul can be renewed. *Solving the Spiritual Dilemma* can in no way profess to impart good judgment or reasoning ability like the library of Books that does: the Holy Bible. The Book of Proverbs is primarily focused on wisdom—a trait which, like discernment, imparts understanding and good judgment. The Bible consists of sixty-six Books, all of which are inspired by the Source of wisdom—our God and Creator.

Reading and comprehending to the end, God's truth is presented in the Scriptures in such a manner that His truth cannot honestly be disputed.

Quoting Peter Kerr from his book, *Election and Predestination*:

> "Anyone who has read the entire Bible has seen that God stands alone as Creator, Master, King, Judge, Sovereign, etc. But on the other hand, within this same Bible, in just as plain language, God commands His created beings, over and over again, to make choices, warning them of negative consequences for wrong choices and promising them positive blessings for right choices."[2]

What is Discernment?

The basic definition of the noun *discernment*:
> "The power or faculty of the mind, by which it distinguishes one thing from another, as truth from falsehood, virtue from vice; acuteness of judgment. ... The errors of youth often proceed from the want of *discernment.*"[3]

Noah Webster also gives the definition of the verb to *discern*:
> To see or understand the difference; to make distinction; as, to *discern* between good and evil, truth and falsehood.[4]

As a youngster matures, the mind is capable of receiving both *sound* and *false* teaching. Noah Webster's 1828 Dictionary gives the definition of *doctrine*:
> In a *general sense*, [doctrine is] whatever is taught. Hence, a principle or position in any science; whatever principle or position is laid down as true by an instructor or master. The *doctrines* of the gospel [from God and spell, means *good news*] are the principles or truths taught by Christ and his apostles. The *doctrines* of Plato are the principles which he taught. Hence a *doctrine* may be true or false; it may be a mere tenet [theory] or opinion.[5]

Consequently, both spiritual and worldly things are correspondingly discovered. Two different individuals, instead of being of one mind, can be of different opinions.

The act of *discerning* is much the same as *detecting*. To detect something is described as:
> "finding out what is concealed, hidden, or formerly unknown. To discover; to find out; to bring to light. The

act of detecting; finding out what is concealed, especially what is concealed by design, hidden, or formerly unknown; discovery."[6]

"To discern is to see or understand differences; to make distinction; to have clearness of mental vision. A discerner makes clear-sighted observations and judgments; and has the power of distinguishing or perceiving differences of things or ideas, and their relations."[7]

Discernment, reasoning, and *wisdom* go hand in hand. Mr. Webster, in his definition of the word *solid,* also said,
"Wise men seek *solid* reasons for their opinions."[8]

It has been said, "The influence of a valid education which is free from error cannot be refuted. When absolute truth is planted, the facts produce a new found power to see what is not evident to all people."

The Lord Jesus instructed His eleven [after Judas Iscariot was no more]:
Sanctify [set those who would believe, apart from the world] through thy truth; thy word is truth. John 17:17

I am [Jesus is] the way, the truth, and the life: no man cometh unto [goes to] the Father [in heaven], but by me. John 14:6b

For my mouth shall speak truth; Proverbs 8:7a

My mouth shall speak of wisdom. Psalm 49:3a

At various times those who are not able to back up their opinions have distorted and attempted to revise history. However, no matter what is said, the *truth* of history never changes. Noah Webster describes the *truth* of history:

> The *truth* of history constitutes its whole value. We rely on the *truth* of the scriptural prophecies.[9]

The word *heart* has a double meaning. It can be referring to the physical heart which is in our chests, or metaphorically like when we hear someone say, "She has a good heart." The *heart*, according to James Strong, when used figuratively, can be a synonym of *mind*, and, in this sense, is regarded as the foundation of discernment, knowledge, and wisdom. James Strong describes the heart:

> "The heart includes not only the motives, feelings, affections, and desires, but also the will, the aims, the principles, the thoughts, and the intellect of man. In fact, it embraces the whole inner man, the head never being regarded as the seat of intelligence. While it is the source of all action and the center of all thought and feeling the heart is also described as receptive to the influences both from the outer world and from God Himself."[10]

Discernment then, as taught by theologian Joseph Rioux, is the *action* of selecting the most excellent decision—the wisest choice—in any and all circumstances. The *best response* is not based on the wisdom of any other created being; rather the unsurpassed answer is the Source of wisdom—life's Creator:

> But of him ye are in Christ Jesus, who of God is made unto us wisdom. 1 Corinthians 1:30a

> For the LORD giveth wisdom: out of his mouth *cometh* knowledge and understanding. Proverbs 2:6

It would seem reasonable that the creature should trust his Creator:

> [2]That their hearts might be comforted [encouraged], being knit together in love, and unto [attaining to] all riches of the full assurance of understanding, to the acknowledgement of the mystery of God, and [both] of the Father, and of Christ; [3]In whom are hid all the treasures of wisdom and knowledge. Colossians 2:2-3

The word *sound* has many definitions, but the one which is much like the word *right* (as in the word *correct*), is used in the Scriptures for *sound doctrine.* The definition of *sound* from Noah Webster:

> "Founded in truth, Right; correct; well founded; free from error."[11]

> Hold fast the form of sound words, which thou hast heard of me, in faith and love which is in Christ Jesus. 2 Timothy 1:13

> For the time will come when they will not endure sound doctrine; but after their own lusts shall they heap to themselves teachers, having itching ears; And they shall turn away *their* ears from the truth, and shall be turned unto fables. 2 Timothy 4:3-4

> Holding fast the faithful word as he hath been taught, that he may be able by sound doctrine both to exhort [encourage] and to convince [convict] the gainsayers [those who contradict]. Titus 1:9

> BUT speak thou the things which become [are proper for] sound doctrine: [2]That the aged men be sober, grave

[reverent], temperate, sound in faith, in charity [love], in patience. Titus 2:1-2

[7]In all things showing thyself a pattern of good works: in doctrine *showing* uncorruptness [integrity], gravity [reverence], sincerity, [8]Sound speech, that cannot be condemned; that he that is of the contrary part [an opponent] may be ashamed, having no evil thing to say of you. Titus 2:7-8

When making decisions on any and all courses of action, the *best response* is to do what pleases—not self—not other people—but what pleases the Lord:

> For do I now persuade men, or God? Or do I seek to please men? For if I yet pleased men, I should not be the servant of Christ." Galatians 1:10

If, instead of preaching the truth, Paul, the apostle, had preached what was pleasing to others just for them to hear what they wanted to hear, he would not have been a worthy servant of the Savior.

> not as pleasing men, but God, which trieth [tests] our hearts. 1 Thessalonians 2:4b

> and do those things that are pleasing in his [God's] sight. 1 John 3:22b

> [3]Yea, if thou criest after knowledge [discernment], *and* liftest up thy voice for understanding; ... [5]Then shalt thou understand the fear [reverential awe] of the LORD, and find the knowledge of God. [6]For the LORD giveth wisdom: out of his mouth *cometh* knowledge and understanding. Proverbs 2:3, 5-6

[7]The works of his [God's] hands *are* verity [truth] and judgment; all his commandments *are* sure. [8]They stand fast for ever and ever, *and are* done in truth and uprightness. ... [9b]holy and reverend *is* his name.
Psalm 111:7-8, 9b

Since God is *holy*—that is, totally *righteous*—and since God is the Source of wisdom and discernment; then to know God is to know what is *right*. Speaking of a man, everything one does, *should be* the *right* thing to do, and should be done in accordance with the authorities' laws *and* the things that are pleasing—not displeasing—to God. When a man does what is within the will of God, then he is doing what is done in accordance with truth.

"God's Law—the Ten Commandments—is the perfect standard of truth and justice. When laws are definite, *right* and *wrong* are easily ascertained and understood."[12]

The definition of *righteous* is
"Just; accordant to the divine law."[13]

Applied to the Lord Jesus, righteousness is holy obedience to the Father with flawless perfection.

"*Applied to persons*, it denotes one who is holy in heart, and observant of the divine commands in *practice*. The *righteous* in Scripture, denote the servants of God, the saints."[14]

The word *saints* in the above quote speaks of everyone who is a true believer. Anyone who believes is set apart from the world (sanctified) and is one of the Lord's *saints*.

***

The author you're reading was still confused about what was true and what was false when he graduated from high school and joined the US Air Force in 1961. Thinking he was a Christian, and that he might get killed, he got baptized by being immersed in a tank of water at a Christian Church. But, not really knowing God, he was not a true, *believing* Christian; he was actually a *professed* Christian. Before he went under the water, he was a dry sinner; and when he came up out of the water, he was a wet sinner. He would later learn that there was nothing—including getting baptized—he could physically do to save himself. This is the reason we are blessed with the Savior's physical work on the cross, shedding His blood to forgive us and dying for us so we can have life in Him.

Two Different Baptisms: Spirit and Water

What does baptism have to do with discernment? The answer: If the only thing anyone needs to do to get to heaven is to get water baptized, then people would be lined up waiting to be baptized in the ocean, a lake, a river, or a baptismal tank. It takes only a little reasoning—that is, discernment—to understand this notion. *If it sounds too good to be true...it probably isn't.*

Being baptized in water does not save a person. However, the importance of the event for a new believer cannot be over-emphasized, but the reason for the baptism must be correctly understood. Upon his acceptance of and believing in God, the new believer is immediately spiritually [invisibly] baptized by Jesus into the Holy Spirit who then forever indwells—that is, abides within—the regenerated person.

> [11a]I [John the Baptist] indeed baptize you with water unto repentance: ... [11c]he [Jesus] shall baptize you with the Holy Ghost... Matthew 3:11a, c

Then soon after being spiritually baptized, the new believer is physically [visibly] water baptized, showing publicly, front and center, an obvious declaration that the Lord Jesus has earlier baptized him by indwelling him—already immersing the Holy Spirit—within his soul. Everyone attending at the subsequent water baptism, sees that he testifies to the fact that he is a changed person, a new creature with a new heart—a new believer in Christ.

> Therefore if any man *be* in Christ, *he is* a new creature: old things are passed away; behold, all things are become new. 2 Corinthians 5:17

> For as many of you as have been baptized into Christ have put on Christ. Galatians 3:27

At the moment a person believes, the Holy Spirit indwells —is absorbed into—his being—Jesus *spiritually* baptizes him, and then he *publicly* "puts on Christ" by being immersed in water baptism. It can be said like this: When a soldier puts on his uniform, he identifies himself as being in the army. When the believer "puts on Christ" he identifies himself as being in Christ.

The two different baptisms, Spirit and water baptisms, will be further expounded upon in chapter three. But first, the enormous, eternal value for one to possess discernment should be noted.

Chapter 2

Discernment – A Matter of Life and Death

Ground-to-ground and ground-to-air communications in the Vietnam conflict required cryptic radio transceivers to prevent the enemy from intercepting vital secret transmissions. When it was necessary to use this means, one of the users would key the radio and say, "Going cipher." Both the sender and the receiver then needed to *plug-in* a device with several pins of authenticated codes. If one or the other did not have the daily authentication to set up their cipher device, then the transmission would be garbled and impossible for the receiving end to *decipher* what was being sent.

Discerning what the Bible tells us is dependent upon being able to *decipher* what our Savior is telling us—or, stated in a different way, being able to *discern* how God wants us to know Him in order to be saved for all eternity. Just like in a war, not deciphering what is being said can have fatal consequences. This vital matter will be further expounded upon in the next chapter.

The end result of people not possessing discernment is that without it utter chaos would prevail. A *standard* criterion of law and order to be observed would provide unity and peace, whereas riots, looting, and killings would erupt if individuals are left to decide upon their own. If each person is allowed to determine for himself what is right or wrong, then there would be an *anything goes* society. The influence of different kinds of peers, music, movies, books, and social media can sway minds in a negative manner just as these same entities can result in persuading actions to lean to positive behavior.

> He that walketh with wise *men* shall be wise: but a companion of fools shall be destroyed. Proverbs 13:20

There are many reasons that we should have abundant enough reasoning ability to decipher truth from falsehood, the most important being the fact that it has everything to do with finding the path to *eternal* life in heaven. Thomas asked Jesus:

> [5b]How can we know the way? [6]Jesus saith unto him, I am the way, the truth, and the life: no man cometh unto the Father, but by me. John 14:5b-6

The Lord Jesus also proclaimed to Nicodemus:

> Jesus answered and said unto him, Verily, verily [Truly, truly], I say unto thee, Except a man be born again, he cannot see the kingdom of God. John 3:3

The everlasting virtue of having and using discernment is that having it gives man the spiritual power to make the most important decision of his life: that which has *eternal* consequences. Jesus, the only begotten Son of God, is again quoted:

> [15]That whosoever believeth in him should not perish, but have eternal life. [16]For God so loved the world [the people—not the planet], that he gave his only begotten Son, that whosoever believeth in him should not

perish, but have everlasting life. [17]For God sent not his Son into the world to condemn the world; but that the world through him might be saved. [18]He that believeth on him is not condemned [to the anger—wrath—fury of God]: but he that believeth not is condemned already, because he hath not believed in the name of the only begotten Son of God. John 3:15-18

He that believeth on the Son hath everlasting life: and he that believeth not the Son shall not see life; but the wrath of God abideth [remains] on him. John 3:36

Verily, verily, I say unto you, He that believeth on me hath everlasting life. John 6:47

But, of the Three Persons of God, is believing in the Son the only One in whom we believe? *Whom exactly* is Jesus speaking of when He says in John 3:16: "whoever *believes* in *Him*?" Who is this *Him*? Is He speaking of Himself or of God the Father who sent Him? The question just **begins** to be answered in John chapter 5:

Verily, verily, I say unto you, He that heareth my word, and believeth *on him* [emphasis added] that sent me, hath everlasting life, and shall not come into condemnation; but is passed from death unto life. John 5:24

Whosoever denieth the Son, the same hath not the Father [but]; *he that acknowledgeth the Son hath the Father also.* 1 John 2:23

Of course, we *also* believe in the Father who sent our Lord Jesus. In fact, we sure enough do believe that God is Three Persons: Father, Son and Holy Spirit. The essence of God includes all Three. We cannot have One without the other Two. They are united, making them all One. The Lord Jesus confirms this when He Himself says this:

I and *my* Father are one. John 10:30

It is essential to have all *Three*; like the essence of *time*. Jabe Nicholson said something like, "To have of *all* of time, we must have *all* three parts of time; 1) *past*, 2) *present*, and 3) *future*. God's Word tells us there are Three who are all the One Almighty God:

For there are three that bear record [witness] in heaven; the Father, the Word [Jesus], and the Holy Ghost [Holy Spirit]: and these three are one. 1 John 5:7

The answer to the question: "Who was Jesus referring to in John 3:16?" The answer is, then: *All Three*. We believe in each One individually AND all Three as *One*—united. We learn that the Spirit is the One who raises us back to everlasting life:

But if the Spirit of him that raised up Jesus from the dead dwell in you, he that raised up Christ from the dead shall quicken [give life to] your mortal bodies by his Spirit that dwelleth in you. Romans 8:11

Looking into the verse of John 3:16, we find there are five verbs. Emphasis is added to point out these predicates—these cause-and-effect expressions:

For God so *loved* the world, that he *gave* his only be-gotten Son, that whosoever *believeth* in him should not *perish*, but *have* everlasting life.

The five verbs, *loved, gave, believeth, perish* and *have*, all together, explain the reason for the Gospel. Jabe Nicholson points out the eternal impact that three of these verbs have on a person's life:

"God the Father *gave*, you *believeth*, so you *have*."

"He *gave*."

"You *believeth*."

"You *have*."

If anyone believes in God without believing in the Son—or, believes in the Son without believing in the Father, the consequence can be the same *Lake of Fire* (known in the Scriptures as the *second death*) as for any unbeliever:

> [22]Who is a liar but he that denieth that Jesus is the Christ? He is antichrist, that denieth the Father and the Son. [23]Whosoever denieth the Son, the same hath not the Father: [but] *he that acknowledgeth the Son hath the Father also.* 1 John 2:22-23

In the Bible there are many other names given to recognize the Lord Jesus. One of these names is *the Word*:

> [1]IN the beginning was the Word, and the Word was with God, and the Word was God...
>
> [14a]And the Word was made flesh, and dwelt among us... John 1:1, 14a

That is the simplicity of the Gospel message. It is that plain. God *gave* us His only begotten Son to take on the punishment in our place for our offenses. God did so, full knowing that He would raise Him back to life from the dead. God believed He could do it, and He wants us to have the same confidence that He will raise those who believe in Him. He wants us to know that He will send His Son back to raise us up if we believe what He is telling us. When we believe that Jesus died for us and lives for us, we will be raised, saved from wrath, to life— when we become convinced, then, indeed, we will be raised and *have* eternal life.

Eternal life comes with simple belief! Wow! It's so simple—and it's free! It does not come from how many times we appear in church, take communion, or perform all the standing up, sitting down, raising our hands, and any number of other rituals and *works* we *do*. There are lots of people in lots of religions who are very *good* people, but God is looking for the ones who know Him and *believe* in Him. He sees our motives. He knows whether we do good deeds to be seen by man, or whether we do good works because of the fact that we are so thankful for God loving us so much that He gave the ultimate sacrifice to save us. We do good works not to save ourselves but we are obedient to do good works—because we are saved!

This is not to take away from the importance of assembling together on the first day of the week for breaking the bread, fellowshipping, praying, and hearing God's truths through the preacher's teaching. These things follow in one's life because of sincere, heartfelt *belief*. Believers are given a hunger to obey, where those who think they do not need the Savior, that is, those who "pay, pray, and obey" believe they can save themselves. If that were so, then Jesus died on the cross for nothing.

People are not saved by doing any number of *good works*. We are saved only by having faith in God that what He says is true. We cannot make ourselves *righteous*. Only God sees us as being righteous, and He only sees us as being righteous when He sees that we believe.

The Lord Jesus says:
> And this is the will of him that sent me, that everyone which seeth the Son, and believeth on him, may have everlasting life: and I will raise him up at the last day. John 6:40

> And this is the record [testimony]: that God hath given to us eternal life, and this life is in His Son. 1 John 5:11

Developing discernment is much the same as developing *belief*. Upon *knowing* the *truth*, we can depend on the facts. We are convinced that it is *indeed* the *truth*.

Anyone who believes can absolutely prove the truth to himself, because he for sure realizes he is a changed person. He knows this to be genuinely, totally certain, because he has undergone a life-changing relationship with Jesus Christ. He no longer allows peer pressure to cause him to deny his belief. Jesus, fully God and fully Man, said:

> For whosoever shall be ashamed of me and of my words, of him shall the Son of man be ashamed, when he shall come in his own glory, and *in his* Father's, and of the holy angels. Luke 9:26

> Yea, let none that wait on thee be ashamed: let them be ashamed which transgress [deal treacherously] without cause. Psalm 25:3

There are many reasons (or excuses) for not believing. Some of these are pride, the want for riches, and hatred for God when some catastrophic event happens and a target of blame needs to be cast. One of the biggest reasons for believing or for *not* believing is that a person becomes knowledgeable of *good* and *evil*. And, hindered by pride, the one who continues to not believe, does not want to admit guilt.

> [3]But of the fruit of the tree which *is* in the midst of the garden, God hath said, Ye shall not eat of it, neither shall ye touch it, lest ye die. [4]And the serpent said unto the woman, Ye shall not surely die: [5]For God doth know that in the day ye eat thereof, then your eyes shall be opened, and ye shall be *as gods* [as God], *knowing good and evil*. Genesis 3:3-5

> For all that is in the world, the lust of the flesh, and the lust of the eyes, and the pride of life, is not of the Father, but is of the world. 1 John 2:16

When people think they do not need any criterion for what is right and what is wrong other than their own personal standard, then the *anything goes* attitude takes over. Being "as gods" would most likely give people a lot of *pride*. As the eyes become open to the things of the world—that is, "the lust of the eyes, the lust of the flesh, and the *pride* of life"—temptations with the temporary earthly pleasures can become unbridled.

> [15]Love not the world, neither the things *that are* in the world. If any man love the world, the love of the Father is not in him. [16]For all that *is* in the world, the lust of the flesh, and the lust of the eyes, and the pride of life, is not of the Father, but is of the world. [17]And the world passeth away, and the lust thereof: but he that doeth the will of God abideth for ever. 1 John 2:15-17

When one *discerns* the difference between good and evil, guilt can set in, and, admittedly, *guiltiness can be very difficult to confess.*

The eternal importance of discerning the truth and holding on to it cannot be overemphasized. Matthew Henry (1662-1714) called false teachers *seducers*:

> "Seducers are more dangerous to the church than persecutors."[15]

Discerning truth from falsehood can be challenging, but having faith that the Bible is absolutely true and staying in the Word can lead to discerning false teaching versus sound doctrine. The word *truth* is in the Bible 235 times. Three examples having to do with truth and its purity are provided in the following Psalms:

> Lead me in thy truth, and teach me: for thou *art* the God of my salvation [the God who saves me]; on thee do I wait all the day. Psalm 25:5

> The words of the LORD *are* pure words: as silver tried in a furnace of earth, purified seven times. Psalm 12:6

> For the LORD *is* good; his mercy *is* everlasting; and his truth *endureth* to all generations. Psalm 100:5

The Book of Proverbs also lends well to the importance of knowing the truth:

> [3]Let not mercy and truth forsake thee: bind them about thy neck; write them upon the table of thine heart; [4]So shalt thou find favor and good understanding [high esteem] in the sight of God and man. Proverbs 3:3-4

> Buy the truth, and sell *it* not; *also* wisdom, and instruction, and understanding. Proverbs 23:23

> [5]Every word of God *is* pure [tried, found pure]: he *is* a shield unto them that put their trust in him. [6]Add thou not unto his words, lest he reprove [convict] thee, and thou be found a liar. Proverbs 30:5-6

***

Since discernment is having good reasoning ability based on what is not falsehood, rather what is *truth*, then created human beings, again, need to turn to the Source of not only wisdom, but also of *truth*. The Creator of *all things* must necessarily be sincerely acknowledged:

All things were made by him; and without him was not anything made that was made. John 1:3

The pronoun *him* (The pronouns for any of the Three Persons of God are not capitalized in the King James Version) in the previous verse is referring to the Lord Jesus Christ. Quoting *him*, the Lord Jesus:

To this end was I born, and for this cause came I into the world, that I should bear witness unto the truth. Every one that is of the truth heareth my voice. John 18:37b

It is wise to know the *truth*. God desires that we *know Him* above all else, because when we *know Him*, then we believe Him. The LORD is quoted:

For I desired mercy [faithfulness, belief], and not sacrifice; and *knowledge* [emphasis added] of God more than burnt offerings. Hosea 6:6

But let him that glorieth glory in this, that he understandeth and knoweth me, that I *am* the LORD which exercise lovingkindness, judgment, and righteousness, in the earth: for in these *things* I delight, saith the LORD. Jeremiah 9:24

Who *is* a God like unto thee, that pardoneth iniquity [wickedness, sin], and passeth by [passes over] the transgression [knowingly sinning] of the remnant [the few who are leftover] of his heritage? He retaineth not his anger for ever, because he delighteth *in* mercy [loving kindness]. Micah 7:18

Jesus is quoted:

> And this is life eternal, that they [Christ's future apostles] might know thee the only true God, and Jesus Christ, whom thou hast sent. John 17:3

> [20]Neither pray I for these alone, but for them also which shall believe on me through their word [apostles' New Testament writings]; [21]That they [those who would come to believe] all may be one as thou, Father, *art* in me, and I in thee, that they also may be one in us: that the world [unbelieving people] may believe that thou hast sent me. John 17:20-21

A most significant part of knowing the truth is to know that Jesus is equally God with the Father and the Holy Spirit:

> IN the beginning was the Word, and the Word was with God, and the Word was God. [2]The same was in the beginning with God... [14]And the Word was made flesh, and dwelt among us, (and we beheld his glory, the glory as of the only begotten of the Father,) full of grace and truth. John 1:1-2, 14

> [14]In whom we have redemption [been repurchased] through his blood, even the forgiveness of sins: [15]Who is the image of the invisible God, the first-born of every creature [*first born* here means *in existence* even before all created things including the universe]: [16]For by him [Jesus] were all things created, that are in heaven, and that are in earth, visible and invisible, whether *they be* thrones, or dominions, or principalities, or powers: all things were created by him, and for him: [17]And he is before all things, and by him all things consist. [18]And he [Jesus] is the head of the body, the church: who is the beginning, the first-born from the dead; that in all

things he might have the pre-eminence. [19]For it pleased *the Father* that in him should all fullness dwell. Colossians 1:14-19

[5]Let this mind be in you, which was also in Christ Jesus: [6]Who, being in the form of God, thought it not robbery to be equal with God: [7]But made himself of no reputation, and took upon him the form of a servant, and was made in the likeness of men: [8]And being found in fashion as a man, he humbled himself, and became obedient unto death, even the death of the cross. [9]Wherefore God also hath highly exalted him, and given him a name which is above every name: [10]That at the name of Jesus every knee should bow, of *things* in heaven, *and things* in earth, and *things* under the earth; [11]And *that* every tongue should confess that Jesus Christ *is* Lord, to the glory of God the Father. Philippians 2:5-11

The Father is quoted in some of the following verses, calling His Son "LORD" and "GOD", and also confirms that His Son [the Lord Jesus Christ] created all things. When the Father is quoted in the KJV Bible, His words are capitalized:

GOD, who at sundry times and in divers manners spake in time past unto the fathers by the prophets, [2]Hath in these last days spoken unto us by *his* Son, whom he hath appointed heir of all things, by whom also he made the worlds; [3]Who being the brightness of *his* glory [Jesus is the glory of His Father] and the express image of his person, and upholding all things by the word of his power, when he had by himself purged our sin, sat down on the right hand of the Majesty on high; [4]Being made so much better than the angels, as he hath by inheritance obtained a more excellent name than they. [5]For unto which of the angels said he at any

time, THOU ART MY SON, THIS DAY HAVE I BEGOT-
TEN THEE? And again, I WILL BE TO HIM A FATHER,
AND HE SHALL BE TO ME A SON? [6]And again, when
he bringeth in the first begotten into the world, he
saith, AND LET ALL THE ANGELS OF GOD WORSHIP
HIM. [7]And of the angels he saith, WHO MAKETH HIS
ANGELS SPIRITS, AND HIS MINISTERS A FLAME OF
FIRE. [8]But unto the Son *he saith*, THY THRONE, O GOD,
IS FOR EVER AND EVER: A SCEPTER [a Ruler's staff]
OF RIGHTEOUSNESS *IS* THE SCEPTER OF THY KING-
DOM. [9]THOU HAST LOVED RIGHTEOUSNESS, AND
HATED INIQUITY; THEREFORE GOD, *EVEN* THY GOD,
HATH ANOINTED THEE WITH THE OIL OF GLAD-
NESS ABOVE THY FELLOWS. [10]And, THOU, LORD, IN
THE BEGINNING HAST LAID THE FOUNDATION OF
THE EARTH; AND THE HEAVENS ARE THE WORKS
OF THINE HANDS. Hebrews 1:1-10

THE heavens declare the glory of God; and the firmament showeth his handiwork. Psalm 19:1

To have *discernment*, and to have *knowledge* of God are both
vital traits. To produce these; sound doctrine is essential. Every one of God's created human beings should be afforded the
opportunity to acquire His truth to have life and not death.

For the wages of sin *is* death; but the gift of God *is* eternal life through Jesus Christ our Lord. Romans 6:23

He that believeth on the Son hath everlasting life: and
he that believeth not the Son shall not see life; but the
wrath of God abideth on him. John 3:36

Certainly, discernment is a matter of life and death. Since
a man is only a created being and cannot *do* anything to save

himself, how can he obtain discernment? Discerning God's Word provides the power to save a person.

The Power of the Gospel Message

> For I am not ashamed of the gospel of Christ: for it is the power of God unto salvation to every one that believeth... Romans 1:16a

How does the Holy Spirit contribute to developing discernment if a person must have belief and already be immersed by the Holy Spirit to indwell him? If an unbeliever must have the Holy Spirit to perceive the Gospel message, but the Holy Spirit only indwells those who believe, how does one overcome this impasse?

Chapter 3

The Discernment Dilemma

To Believe a Matter is True...You Must Hear the Proof
BUT
To Hear the Proof of a Matter...You Must Believe it is True

What Power enables a person to *hear*—that is, to understand—to comprehend what is written or spoken of?

To *possess* spiritual discernment, one must have the Spirit residing within his soul and mind [be indwelled by the Spirit], in order to *attain* spiritual discernment. The power of God's Word is what saves a person. But, if a person cannot understand Spiritual things from God's Word, then the Spirit will not be abiding within him. Read that again. Think about it. A perfect example of this is pointed out thus: *Faith*—or the acceptance of something being true—in a word, *believing*—comes from an indisputable Source:

> So then faith *cometh* by hearing, and hearing [the saving Gospel message] by the word of God. Romans 10:17

That verse says that one acquires faith by *hearing*—by *understanding* the Scriptures which are of the Spirit of God. Yet, if a person does not *believe* in God (or does not have *faith* in Him) and hence does not have the indwelling Spirit of God, it is not possible to understand God's Word which is what produces the faith in the first place.

> But the natural [unbelieving, unsaved] man receiveth not the things of the Spirit of God: for they are foolishness unto him: neither can he know *them*, because they are spiritually discerned. 1 Corinthians 2:14

To the question of why the Pharisees could not understand His Words, Jesus explained by telling them they *could not* be listening. He let them know like this:

> Why do ye not understand my speech? *even* because ye cannot hear my word. John 8:43

Then the Savior went on to say:

> He that is of God heareth God's words: ye therefore hear *them* not, because ye are not of God. John 8:47

The dilemma is further amplified by the fact that all Scripture is inspired by God. So, in order for a person to understand Scripture, he must have within himself the Holy Spirit of God, and the Holy Spirit does not indwell anyone until the moment the person becomes a believer.

Of course, this dilemma of not already having the Spirit can lead one to think then that it is impossible to be saved. However, Scripture does not stop with only one or two verses. *All* of God's Word needs to be considered in order to keep it *all* in *context*.

> the holy scriptures, which are able to make thee wise unto salvation through faith which is in Christ Jesus. All

scripture is given by inspiration of God,
2 Timothy 3:15b-16a

How then shall thy call on him in whom they have not
believed? and how shall they believe in him of whom
they have not heard? and how shall they hear without a
preacher? Romans 10:14

But if our gospel be hid [veiled], it is hid to them that
are lost [perishing]. 2 Corinthians 4:3

The Gospel, which a true servant of God proclaims, is the
true teaching of the glorious Savior who gave His life to offer
eternal life to those who believe in the Son of God the Father.

So then faith *cometh* by hearing, and hearing by the
word of God. Romans 10:17

After—or upon—the moment of first *believing* in the Son of
God to be the Savior, then *understanding* what God's Word is
saying, becomes possible:

[Christ] in whom ye also *trusted*, after that ye heard
[understood] the word of truth, the gospel of your salvation: in whom also after that ye believed, ye were sealed
with that Holy Spirit of promise. Ephesians 1:13

ye [you] received [welcomed] *it* [the Word of God] not
as the word of men, but as is in truth, the word of God,
which effectually [effectively] worketh [worked] also in
you that believe. 1 Thessalonians 2:13b

Paraphrasing Warren Henderson's explanation:
The world says, "I believe when I see." But the spiritual
man proclaims, "I see when I believe."[16]

If no one points out the Gospel message in God's Scripture to a lost soul, how can a worldly, guilt ridden man ever know that Christ Jesus poured out His blood to forgive him? How will the undeserving unbeliever know that Jesus, in His own body on the cross, took on the unbeliever's punishment? And how would he even know Christ was raised back to life from the dead to give the unbeliever hope to also be eternally resurrected and saved from the wrath to come? If no one tells him, how would he know that he is indeed not saved by being lost in his thinking he could save himself by being *good*—by doing good deeds—or good works? He needs to hear from someone or from reading about it that he is saved from wrath and for everlasting life *only* by God's *grace*. Man cannot save himself:

Not of works, lest any man should boast. Ephesians 2:9

I do not frustrate [set aside, forget about] the grace of God: for if righteousness *come* by the law [by me doing good works], then Christ is dead in vain [then Christ died for nothing]. Galatians 2:21

People, who have been saved, do good works *not to save themselves*—rather they do good works *because they have already been saved*!

For we are his workmanship [His creation], created in Christ Jesus unto [for] good works, Ephesians 2:10a

[5]Not by works of righteousness which we have done, but according to his mercy he saved us, by the washing of regeneration, and renewing of the Holy Ghost [Holy Spirit]; [6]Which he shed on us abundantly through Jesus Christ our Savior; [7]That being justified by his grace, we should be made heirs according to the hope of eternal life. Titus 3:5-7

All of our bodies are guaranteed to die at some point: so then, what are we saved *from*?

> And as it is appointed unto men once to die [to die one time], but after this the judgment. Hebrews 9:27

Death cannot be what believers are saved *from* if, in fact, all—both believers and nonbelievers—are going to die. So that which believers are saved *from* is this: Believers souls will not *suffer* in their graves (Hādēs). Believers are saved from God's wrath and from the *second death* which is eternal suffering in the Lake of Fire.

On the other hand, the souls of those who have rejected the Savior will also be resurrected from having suffered a miserable time in their graves, but not to be saved from the Lake of Fire. They will be raised to face the Lord for final judgment and second death in which their dying never ends.

> And many of them that sleep in the dust of the earth shall awake, some to everlasting life, and some to shame *and* everlasting contempt. Daniel 12:2

The heartbreaking, abhorrent judgment will be only for the unbelieving at the end of Christ's Millennial reign, and it will take place at the Great White Throne Judgment. John prophesied the end times in *The Revelation of Jesus Christ*—the last Book in the Bible:

> [12a]And I saw the dead, small and great, stand before God; ... [12c]and the dead were judged out of those things which were written in the books, according to their works [God's records will clearly show that they were guilty sinners who did not repent]. Revelation 20:12a, c

> And death and hell [Hādēs] were cast into the lake of fire. This is the second death. Revelation 20:14

This is not to say that believers are *holier than thou* in man's view. All of us have a past history that we're not proud of. The only difference is that believers have *admitted* to God that they have sinned against Him and are genuinely sorry and have repented:

> Wherefore, as by one man [Adam] sin entered into the world, and death by sin; and so death passed upon all men, for that all have sinned: Romans 5:12

We all experience the first death, but the *second* death is reserved for the unrepentant:

> For the wages of sin *is* death; but the gift of God *is* eternal life through Jesus Christ our Lord. Romans 6:23

The Beginning of Restoration

From Ruined – To Rescued – And Restored

RUINED
Photo Credit: Chris Gentry

RUINED
Photo Credit: Chris Gentry

For all have sinned, and come short of
the glory of God.
Romans 3:23

RESCUED
Photo Credit: Chris Gentry

RESCUED
Photo Credit: Chris Gentry

Behold, now *is* the day of salvation.
2 Corinthians 6:2b

RESTORED
Photo Credit: Chris Gentry

Therefore if any man *be* in Christ, *he is*
a new creature.
2 Corinthians 5:17a

Before Chris Gentry chose to give life again to the car pictured above, he obviously pictured an enormous amount of work that would have to be done. Then with all that effort and hard work, what he produced was a near perfect, spotless new creation. However, it wasn't free. Chris had to have lots of perseverance, resolve, and determination; and he had to pay for the junked car and for some parts and primer and paint. And, oh what a beautiful end result!

When God looked at our past unbelieving, unlikely to be saved souls, He had already sent His Son to do all the work to save us. There was no more *work* to be done on our part. The Savior's work was done when he died that horrific death on the cross. In a sense, He took that *second death* in our place. Only God could have resurrected Him back to eternal life from the dead. That is the *power* of God. For us, He made it so *simple*. Now, all we need to do is to believe it was so. And the renewed life is *free*. Jesus paid the price. And oh what a beautiful end result!

He restoreth my soul: Psalm 23:3a

[10]Create in me a clean heart, O God; and renew a right spirit within me. Restore unto me the joy of thy salvation; and uphold me *with* thy free [generous] spirit. Psalm 51:10, 12

The LORD is quoted:
And I will give them one heart, and I will put a new spirit within you; and I will take the stony heart out of their flesh, and will give them a heart of flesh: Ezekiel 11:19

[26]A new heart also will I give you, and a new spirit will I put within you: and I will take away the stony heart out of your flesh, and I will give you a heart of flesh. [27]And I will put my spirit within you, and cause you to walk

in my statutes [to do good works], and ye shall keep my judgments, and do *them.* Ezekiel 36:26-27

Restored My Soul
Photo Credit: Chris Gentry

Restored My Soul
Photo Credit: Chris Gentry

He restoreth my soul:
Psalm 23:3a

In God's view, even though believers are still sinners, the Holy Spirit within them, keeps them from *practicing* sin. The Spirit guides believers to quickly recognize their errors and ask for forgiveness. The Spirit then keeps them on a straighter path. The believer is not at all *perfect*. However, in God's view, He sees believers as keeping His statutes—not for self-glory, but as His representatives—for His glory:

> he leadeth me in the paths of righteousness for his name's sake. Psalm 23:3b

> Now then we [believers] are ambassadors for Christ... 2 Corinthians 5:20a

> [13]And ye shall know that I *am* the LORD, when I have opened your graves, O my people, and brought you up out of your graves, [14]And shall put my spirit in you, and ye shall live, and I shall place you in your own land [for believers, our own promised land is heaven]: then shall ye know that I the LORD have spoken *it*, and performed *it*, saith the LORD. Ezekiel 37:13-14

THERE was a man of the Pharisees, named Nicodemus, a ruler of the Jews: ...

> [3]Jesus answered and said unto him, Verily, verily [truly, truly], I say unto thee, Except a man be born again [from above], he cannot see the kingdom of God. ...
> [7]Marvel not that I said unto thee, Ye must be born again. John 3:1, 3, 7

> Being born again, not of corruptible [perishable] seed, but of incorruptible [imperishable], by the word of God, which liveth and abideth for ever. 1 Peter 1:23

It can be seen from the above various writers that they are all in miraculous agreement with one another. It has been said, "Text without context is pretext." In other words, if only one verse is read and not compared to other Scripture to confirm its truth, then it is not necessarily true. Hence, it is only *text*.

By standing alone, a verse can easily be misinterpreted. It is not necessarily truth until God's original intent is discerned—correctly taken to mean what God intended. When God's Word is kept in context, one will see that within the Bible, there are *no* inconsistencies—no contradictions. One verse cannot, and will not, contradict any other part of the sixty-six Books. God's Word is all in miraculous agreement with itself.

> All Scripture *is* given by inspiration of God, and *is* profitable for doctrine [teaching], for reproof [conviction], for correction, for instruction in righteousness.
> 2 Timothy 3:16

Belief begins by realizing that you have committed a sin against God and with your curiosity of seeking the truth. At the moment a person first believes in God, he becomes conscious of a hunger to know more about God. The hunger is satisfied by getting to know who God is. The character and nature of God is found by reading, hearing, understanding, absorbing, and digesting the Word of God—the Holy Bible.

So belief begins with seeking to know God, and when the seeker finds Him, he will believe and be saved. Luke, the writer of Acts, quotes the LORD from what He spoke to Joel the prophet in Joel 2:32. In the KJV, Old Testament verses are quoted with all capitalization:

> AND IT SHALL COME TO PASS, *THAT* WHOSOEVER SHALL CALL ON THE NAME OF THE LORD SHALL BE SAVED. Acts 2:21 (Joel 2:32)

Paul the apostle quotes the LORD in the Book of Romans from the same Joel message:

> For WHOSOEVER SHALL CALL UPON THE NAME OF THE LORD SHALL BE SAVED. Romans 10:13 (Joel 2:32)

Jeremiah prophesied that a person who sincerely seeks the LORD will find the LORD:

> [10a]For thus saith the LORD, ... [11]For I know the thoughts that I think toward you, saith the LORD, thoughts of peace, and not of evil [calamity], to give you an expected end [a future and a hope]. [12]Then shall ye call upon me, and ye shall go and pray unto me, and I will hearken unto [listen to] you. [13]And ye shall seek me, and find *me*, when ye shall search for me with all your heart. [14a]And I will be found of you, saith the LORD: and I will turn [bring you back from] captivity [being captured in the slavery of sin]. Jeremiah 29:10a, 11-14a

The Lord Jesus, in relation to the discernment dilemma, said:

> *Even* the Spirit of truth; whom the world cannot receive, because it seeth him not, neither knoweth him: but ye know him; for he dwelleth with you, and shall be in you. John 14:17

Not all believers have the same degree of understanding, but all believers do have the ability to discern the Spirit of truth—the saving Gospel message. All believers receive some gifts from the Holy Spirit of God, and one of the gifts is the *discerning of spirits*:

> [7]But the manifestation of the Spirit is given to every man to profit withal [all] [8a]For to one is given by the Spirit the word of wisdom ... 1 Corinthians 12:7-8a [10b]to another discerning of spirits.
> 1 Corinthians 12:10b

The importance of the gift of *discerning of spirits* cannot be over emphasized. John the apostle points out the danger of not detecting false spirits when we hear someone who is spreading false teaching—that is, false doctrine:

> BELOVED, believe not every spirit, but try [test] the spirits whether they are of God: because many false prophets [false preachers] are gone out into the world.
> 1 John 4:1

The Entryway to Heaven

So then, delving deeper into sound doctrine—the reliable, flawless, trustworthy Word of God—we come to the *first step* to developing spiritual discernment and the ability to receive the indwelling Spirit of God whereby a person can overcome the dilemma.

This first step is to unlock the doorway to heaven. But what is it that makes this door so difficult to open?

> Because narrow *is* the gate and difficult *is* the way which leads to life, and there are few who find it. Matthew 7:14 NKJV

But why? What is it that makes it so hard?—and yet it is so simple.

What is it that leads people to the entryway to eternal life, but prevents them from opening the door? Is it *pride* that stops a person from taking that first step? Could it be just four little three-word sentences that are so awkward and challenging for men to utter?

In the author's opinion (having been there), it is *guilt*. It is being guilty with too much *pride* to admit the guilt.

"I am guilty." This is the first, simple, little three-word sentence. Who wants to say that? And what would prompt a person to say such a thing? It takes a lot of intestinal fortitude to own up to guilt. But when one is truly being honest with oneself and reads the Ten Commandments, there is no one other than the Lord Jesus who's ever been able to obey all ten. Like it or not, all the rest of us are *guilty*. When we learn that the punishment is separation from God, for *eternal* suffering in the Lake of Fire; and realizing that Christ Jesus took that horrendous scourging punishment, and was nailed to the cross in our place; this should give each of us good reason to contemplate hearing God's truth: *sound doctrine*. Breaking even one of God's Commandments and not sincerely repenting and not asking God's forgiveness will result in the guilty person's suffering in the Lake of Fire. Following are the Ten Commandments which God has given us:

1. "Thou shalt have no other gods before me." Exodus 20:3
2. [4]"Thou shalt not make unto thee any graven image, or any likeness *of any thing* that *is* in heaven above, or that *is* in the earth beneath, or that *is* in the water under the earth: [5a]Thou shalt not bow down thyself to [worship, commit idolatry with] them, nor serve them [idols]: for I the LORD thy God *am* a jealous God" Exodus 20:4-5a
3. "Thou shalt not take the name of the LORD thy God in vain" Exodus 20:7a
4. "Remember the sabbath day [a day of worship], keep it holy." Exodus 20:8
5. "Honor thy father and thy mother" Exodus 20:12
6. "Thou shalt not kill [murder; intentionally take a human life]." Exodus 20:13
7. "Thou shalt not commit adultery [any form of immoral sex]." Exodus 20:14
8. "Thou shalt not steal [no matter what the value]." Exodus 20:15
9. "Thou shalt not bear false witness [tell a lie] against thy neighbor" Exodus 20:16

10. [17a]"Thou shalt not covet thy neighbor's house, thou shalt not covet thy neighbor's wife... [17c]nor anything that *is* thy neighbor's." Exodus 20:17a, c

> *Neighbor* in this case can be "a person with whom one associates regularly or casually without establishing close relations."[17]

> *Neighbor* can also be "One of the human race; any one that needs our help, or to whom we have an opportunity of doing good."[18]

These Ten Commandments are God's Law, and they are what make every person aware that they are *guilty* by having committed any offense [sin] against His Law:

> for by the law [the Commandments] *is* the knowledge of sin. Romans 3:20b

> For whosoever shall keep the whole law, and yet offend in one *point*, he is guilty of all. James 2:10

God deserves our utmost respect for the unconditional love He offered—that of giving His only begotten Son to shed His blood, to die for us, and to give us hope by raising Jesus back to life from the dead—to *eternal life*. We need to know and to revere God for His righteous judgment of each of us. Justice and mercy meet at the cross. He promises to give us eternal life in heaven when we stop rejecting the Savior and accept His free offer:

> [9]He sent redemption unto his people: he hath commanded his covenant for ever: holy and reverend [awesome] *is* his name. [10]The fear of the LORD *is* the beginning of wisdom: a good understanding have all

they that do *his commandments*: his praise endureth for ever. Psalm 111:9-10

The Lord Jesus *obeyed all of God's Commandments* for us— and *as us*. When a person sincerely believes in God, the Father views the believer as having the righteousness of His Son Jesus Christ.

[21a]But now the righteousness of God...

[22a]even the righteousness of God *which is* by faith of Jesus Christ unto all and upon all them that believe. Romans 3:21a, 22a.

The conclusion then, for the first step in opening the door, is to say:

1) I am guilty

I will confess my transgressions unto the LORD. Psalm 32:5b

For I will declare mine iniquity. Psalm 38:18a

Three other three-word sentences in addition to "*I am guilty*" are equally difficult for us to utter: This next one is really easier said than done and is also inhibited by *pride*. But once a person gets past that obstacle, everything starts to get better. The three-word sentence:

2) "I am sorry."

Only by pride cometh contention [argument, strife, conflict]: but with the well advised *is* wisdom [By pride comes nothing but contention]. Proverbs 13:10

Pride *goeth* before destruction, and a haughty [proud, arrogant, self-important attitude] spirit before a fall [spiritual stumbling]. Proverbs 16:18

> A man's pride shall bring him low: but honor shall uphold the humble in spirit [Or, the humble in spirit will retain honor]. Proverbs 29:23

> I will be sorry for my sin. Psalm 38b

> For ye were made sorry after [according to] a godly manner. 2 Corinthians 7:9b

To whom would we be willing to tell we are *sorry*? The most probable person would be someone who means a whole lot to you—someone who loves you very much—and someone whom you love, too. If you have offended someone who loves you, that person wants to hear your sincere apology. And if you do say, "I am sorry," you will probably want to be sincerely forgiven.

The Lord Jesus loves you so greatly; He even laid down His life for you when you offended Him by breaking His Commandment. He genuinely wants you to repent and to hear you say, "I am sorry."

Again, by *pride* getting in the way, the third three-word sentence can also be extremely difficult to express:

3) "I forgive you."

But God forgives instantly when we, with a sincere heart, ask to be forgiven. And He teaches us to be able to forgive others.

> But he [God], being full of compassion, forgave *their* iniquity. Psalm 78:38a

> For thou, Lord, *art* good, and ready to forgive, and plenteous in mercy unto all them that call upon thee. Psalm 86:5

The Lord Jesus said:

> For if ye forgive men their trespasses, your heavenly Father will also forgive you. Matthew 6:14

Pride is a powerful preventive force. But when these three-word sentences are stated, it can make the weight of the world come off the shoulders of both participants.

And if the one who is forgiving is also sincere and does it instantly, and chooses to not hold a grudge nor to remember the offense, then the guilty one becomes conscious of the undeniable, heartfelt love—a love so strong that both parties want to race to see who can say the last little, momentous three words (The Lord Jesus Christ has already won the race):

4) "I love you."

> God is love; and he that dwelleth in love dwelleth in God, and God in him. 1 John 4:16b

> We love him, because he first loved us. 1 John 4:19

The Lord Jesus Christ wants to hear you, in sincerity, say to Him and to each other, "I love you."

> [7]Beloved, let us love one another: for love is of God; and every one that loveth is born of God, and knoweth God. [8]He that loveth not knoweth not God; for God is love. [9]In this was manifested [revealed] the love of God toward us, because that God sent his only begotten Son into the world, that we might live through him. [10]Herein is love, not that we loved God, but that he loved us, and sent his Son *to be* the propitiation for our sins. [11]Beloved, if God so loved us, we ought also to love one another. 1 John 4:7-11

Propitiation in verse ten of that passage means whoever believes he is forgiven by Christ's shed blood has *satisfied*

God's anger so thoroughly, that He forgives and chooses to not remember.

The Lord our God is quoted (again, in the KJV, Old Testament quotes capitalized:

> FOR I WILL BE MERCIFUL TO THEIR UNRIGHTEOUS-NESS, AND THEIR SINS AND THEIR INIQUITIES [lawless deeds] WILL I REMEMBER NO MORE.
> Hebrews 8:12 (Jeremiah 31:34)

Upon receiving the Lord's immediate forgiveness, the Holy Spirit instantly indwells [baptizes, immerses Himself within] the new born man. The believer is then commanded to be water baptized and should respond to the nudge of the Spirit to obey.

Understanding Today's Two Baptisms

First: Baptism by Jesus with the indwelling Holy Spirit

The end of Chapter One promised further explanation of the two baptisms:

The first baptism—the one with which the Holy Spirit indwells a person—is when Satan has lost the battle for the believer's soul. The Lord Jesus said that He had many things to say, but His disciples were not ready to bear more at that time. Then He said:

> Howbeit [However] when he, the Spirit of truth is come, he will guide you into all truth: for he shall not speak of himself [on His own authority]; but whatsoever he shall hear, *that* shall he speak: and he will show you things to come. John 16:13

When the Spirit has inspired a person to sincerely admit *guilt* to having broken at least one or more of God's Commandments, and he is genuinely *remorseful* for it; this is called *repenting*. The very first time the Lord Jesus is quoted in the Gospel According to Mark, He says:

> The time is fulfilled, and the kingdom of God is at hand: repent ye, and believe the gospel. Mark 1:15

> And be not conformed to this world: but be ye transformed by the renewing of your mind, that ye may prove what *is* that good, and acceptable, and perfect, will of God. Romans 12:2

To repent is to turn away from the way of the natural world and go the opposite direction: toward God—to want to know who He *is* who created you and loves you so much. God wants to reunite you with Himself. He wants to restart your life. The Lord Jesus said:

> [6]That which is born of the flesh is flesh; and that which is born of the Spirit is spirit. [7]Marvel not that I said unto thee, Ye must be born again. John 3:6-7

God is quoted:

> And ye shall seek me, and find *me*, when ye shall search for me with all your heart. Jeremiah 29:13

When we find Him, He redeems us back to Himself. And God says:

> [26]A new heart also will I give you, and a new spirit will I put within you: and I will take away the stony heart out of your flesh, and I will give you a heart of flesh. [27]And I will put my spirit within you, and cause you to walk in my statutes, and ye shall keep my judgments, and do *them*. Ezekiel 36:26-27

This new heart and new spirit is what signifies that the believer is *born again*. And thus, the *discernment is acquired* and will continue to be nurtured as the new believer grows in the new-born relationship with the Lord Jesus Christ.

> [10]Create in me a clean heart, O God; and renew a right spirit within me. [11]Cast me not away from thy presence; and take not thy Holy Spirit from me. Psalm 51:10-11

The Son of God said:

> [23]But the hour cometh, and now is, when the true worshipers shall worship the Father in spirit and in truth: for the Father seeketh such to worship him. [24]God *is* a Spirit: and they that worship him must worship *him* in spirit and truth. John 4:23-24

> But the Comforter [Helper (the Holy Spirit)], *which is* the Holy Ghost, whom the Father will send in my name [In John 15:26, the Father delegates His Son to send the Spirit], he shall teach you all things, and bring all things to your remembrance, whatsoever I have said unto you. John 14:26

> But when the Comforter [Helper (Holy Spirit)] is come, whom I will send unto you from the Father, *even* the Spirit of truth, which proceedeth [continually proceeds] from the Father, he shall testify of me: John 15:26

> It is the spirit that quickeneth [gives life]; the flesh profiteth nothing: the words that I speak unto you, *they* are spirit, and *they* are life. John 6:63

God does not change. He is living. He and His living Word have endured many cultures. Culture cannot change God's Word, rather God's Word changes cultures.

For I *am* the LORD, I change not. Malachi 3:6a

Jesus Christ the same yesterday, and today, and for ever. Hebrews 13:8

BUT THE WORD OF THE LORD ENDURETH FOR EVER. And this is the word which by the gospel is preached unto you. 1 Peter 1:25

For the word of God *is* quick [living], and powerful. Hebrews 4:12a

Second: Physical Baptism by Immersion in Water

The second baptism—by water—represents the spiritual unification with Christ in His death and resurrection: The now saved, Spirit indwelt person going under the water *symbolizes* the believer dying with Christ:

> [7]For he that is dead is freed from sin. [8]Now if we be dead with Christ, we believe that we shall also live with him. Romans 6:7-8

When the person being baptized is raised back up from under the water it symbolizes him being raised to life just as Jesus was actually resurrected from the dead:

> Knowing that Christ being raised from the dead dieth no more; death hath no more dominion over him. Romans 6:9

Eternal life has already begun for the new believer having accepted the Savior and instantly receiving the indwelling Spirit upon having belief. Nothing can change it.

> In whom ye also *trusted*, after that ye heard [discerned] the word of truth, the gospel of your salvation: in whom

also after that ye believed, ye were sealed with that holy Spirit of promise. Ephesians 1:13

To acknowledge the unconditional love of Christ for having suffered and died on the cross for him, the new believer returns a deep, sincere love by becoming obedient to do things the way God's Word tells him. The commands of the Lord's hand-chosen apostles are to be obeyed. (2 Peter 3:2). The first step of obedience is to be water baptized. Peter an apostle of Jesus Christ (2 Peter 3:1-2) commanded it:

[44]While Peter yet spake these words, the Holy Ghost fell on all them which heard the word...

[48a]And he commanded them to be baptized in the name of the Lord. Acts 1:44, 48a

Jesus said to His twelve disciples the following, but it applies to all believers for them to at least *practice* obedience:

If ye love me, keep my commandments. John 14:15

When Jesus was asked by a Jewish scribe which of the Commandments was the greatest, He said:

[30]AND THOU SHALT LOVE THE LORD THY GOD WITH ALL THY HEART, AND WITH ALL THY SOUL, AND WITH ALL THY MIND, AND WITH ALL THY STRENGTH: this is the first commandment. [31]And the second *is* like, *namely* this, THOU SHALT LOVE THY NEIGHBOR AS THYSELF. There is none other commandment greater than these. Mark 12:30-31

When a person becomes a believer, he loves the Lord and desires to obey Him.

For in that he died, he died unto sin once [Christ died one time for all sinners]: but in that he liveth, he liveth unto God. Romans 6:10

Since God the Savior lives to serve God the Father, and the believer lives *with Him*, the new Christian also lives to serve God.

The Jewish chief priests attempted to challenge Jesus' authority. But Jesus responded with what was a perplexing question to them—and a perfect answer to the two baptisms for us:

> The baptism of John, whence [which] was it? from heaven, or of men? Matthew 21:25a

The baptism from heaven is the baptism of the Holy Spirit whom is sent by Jesus to indwell believers.

John's baptism of repentance was a baptism by a man on earth—not from heaven. This earthly baptism occurred prior to the Holy Spirit's baptizing the beginning Church. John the Baptist was baptizing people who were repentant of their sins in order to be prepared to meet the soon coming Savior. In a later time, in the beginning of the Book of Acts, the order began in reverse of what transpired later in the Book: The Spirit baptism happened *before* the water baptism. The repentance still took place prior to the Spirit baptism. Jesus, through the Spirit, is the One who gives a new heart and a new spirit. Hence, the brand new believer is a *born again* Christian:

> Therefore if any man *be* in Christ, *he is* a new creature: old things are passed away; behold, all things are become new. 2 Corinthians 5:17

"All things are become new:" New things have *come to be.* There is new understanding—beginning the *discernment* of the things of God.

Being saved is not done by *any* works that *we* do. Our being saved is done by having faith, by believing the works which the Lord Jesus Christ did when He died in the offender's [sinner's] place—on the cross. He Himself took that punishment for the sinners' offenses. Believing these truths to be absolutely true produces the faith that results in a person being saved from *eternal* punishment: True belief encompasses the following: The punishment Jesus underwent for us was horrendous. He was beaten, whipped, and nailed to a wooden cross until dead, was buried in a tomb, and was raised back to *eternal* life three days later. And, as He ascended and returned to heaven, He was seen by eleven of His soon-to-be apostles, and He promises to return for us.

> And when he [Jesus] had spoken these things, while they beheld [watched], he was taken up; and a cloud received him out of their sight. Acts 1:9

But how can anyone convince anyone else to believe? It's like exclaiming to a person who is uptight, anxious, and stressed: "Relax!" and expecting them to instantly calm down. We just don't have that kind of power or control over others.

In the development of discernment we have seen the answer of what the first steps are—to admit our guilt and repent, but then, we need to get to know God. The LORD said:

> For I desired mercy [faithfulness], and not sacrifice [not works]; and the knowledge of God more than burnt offerings. Hosea 6:6

> [8]For by grace are ye saved through faith; and that not of yourselves: *it is* the gift of God: [9]Not of works, lest any man should boast. Ephesians 2:8-9

If we could physically do anything to save ourselves, then we could boast that we do not need the Savior. It would be like saying, "I don't need the Savior Jesus—I can save myself." If that were true, Jesus died for nothing.

> I do not frustrate [set aside] the grace of God: for if righteousness *come* by the law [by boasting that I never

broke a Commandment], then Christ is dead in vain [then Jesus died for nothing]. Galatians 2:21

Our God and Savior loves us so much that He shed His very own blood to forgive us and, in our place, suffered the death of being scourged and nailed to that cross. Yet, some people do not even give it another thought—they just don't care about what He has gone through or about the eternal life He offers for anyone who will accept Him.

When a man swallows his pride, admits his guilt, and sincerely asks to be forgiven, then by the Savior's shed blood, the man is redeemed to be forever no longer separated from God.

Why Do Some Teach that Water Baptism Saves?

Scripture, if not compared to other Scripture, or if not read with the original intent, one can be led to dwell on a verse without realizing it is contradicting other verses.

> Study [be diligent] to show thyself approved unto God, a workman that needeth not to be ashamed, rightly dividing the word of truth. 2 Timothy 2:15

> [The LORD said (Mal. 2:16)] BEHOLD, I will send my messenger [John the Baptist], and he shall prepare the way before me. Malachi 3:1a

John the Baptist was baptizing those who were seeking the Lord with the baptism of repentance, preparing their hearts to meet the Messiah—God the Savior.

The Book of Acts chronologically covers a period of about thirty-three years (circa AD33 - AD66). Since the Jews had only known about *water baptism*, as time progressed, the reason for water baptism progressed from being water baptized before the realization of the Holy Spirit, and subsequently changed to receiving the Holy Spirit and then being water baptized afterwards. Baptism began with John the Baptist before the Church began at Pentecost. This same John said to the Jews whom he was baptizing:

> [11a]I indeed baptize you with water unto repentance: but he [Jesus] that cometh after me is mightier than I ... [11c]he shall baptize you with the Holy Ghost, and *with* fire. Matthew 3:11a, 11c

Only unbelievers will be baptized with fire, because that is the baptism of judgment. But Jesus does indeed baptize believers with the Holy Spirit.

The Lord Jesus said to His eleven soon to be apostles whom had already been water baptized by John the Baptist:

> For John truly baptized with water; but ye shall be baptized with the Holy Ghost not many days from now. Acts 1:5

John's baptism of repentance is what began the baptism sequence that we read of in the early part of Acts:

> Then Peter said unto them [the Jews], Repent, and be baptized every one of you in the name of Jesus Christ for the remission [forgiveness] of sins; and ye shall receive the gift of the Holy Ghost. Acts 2:38

Hence, for the Jewish Christians the order was
1) *Repentance*
2) *Water Baptism*
3) *Holy Spirit.*
But as time progressed for those thirty-three years in the Book of Acts, the sequence changed.

In Acts 8:12-17, when Philip preached the things of God to Simon the sorcerer and some people of Samaria:

1) They *believed*
2) They were baptized in water
3) The apostles prayed for them and laid hands on them
4) They received the Holy Spirit.

Then, in Acts 10:44-48 when the Holy Spirit fell upon *Gentiles* who heard Peter,

1) They had faith, trusted, *believed* the truth, and repented
2) They received the Holy Spirit
3) Then, in obedience, they were water baptized.

This order of events in Acts 10 is what applies to all Church believers today.[19]

The majority of Jews at this present day continue to reject the truth. The Book of Acts transitions from the Jews generally, repeatedly rejecting Christ, to the Gentiles being the ones who receive the Savior. Due to their rebellion and stubbornness, God will keep the unbelieving Jewish blinded until right after the Church is raptured (Romans 11:25-26).

Chapter 4

What is Redemption?

Between the time of conception up to the moment of becoming *accountable* for having carried out an offense against God—an iniquity called sin—the innocent young person is not separated from God. But upon committing that first answerable sin, God then separates that soul from Himself until the person believes in Him, sincerely repents, and asks God to forgive him. At that moment, the person is forgiven and restored to being at one—the sins are atoned for—with God. Redemption, then, is the purchasing back of a person who was at one time at one with God, then lost that relationship, and later was redeemed by a ransom payment:

> [The Lord Jesus Christ] In whom we have redemption through his blood, the forgiveness of sins, according to the riches of his grace: Ephesians 1:7

Believers, who had been separated from God by their offenses toward Him, are repurchased to be back at one with God by the Purchaser: the Savior. The past sins are atoned for by His shed blood, and the sinner is viewed by God as having

God's righteousness—growing to be Christlike. But all true believers know well that they still have Adam's DNA. Just from
evil thoughts that Satan frequently sneaks into their minds,
the Spirit reminds them that they need to clear their con-
sciences and clean their hearts—no less than once a week.

All true Christians are called God's universal Church—and
Jesus purchased each and every one of them with His blood:

> feed the church of God, which he [Jesus] hath purchased
> with his own blood. Acts 20:28b

Redemption is the freedom from our slavery in our offenses
against God. The ransom was paid for by Christ's shed blood,
while nailed through His hands and feet to the cross.

> "Redemption is then the purchase of God's favor by
> the death and sufferings of Christ; the ransom or de-
> liverance of sinners from the bondage of sin and the
> penalties of God's violated law by the atonement of
> Christ."[20]

Believers are *spiritually* redeemed to being again in fellowship with God, but the full deliverance will not take place until
we are *physically* in His presence. Our physical rescue will be
completed when He takes us up to be in heaven face-to-face
with Him.

> [Christ] [13]In whom ye also *trusted*, after that ye heard
> the word of truth, the gospel of your salvation: in whom
> also after that ye believed, ye were sealed with that holy
> Spirit of promise, [14]Which is the earnest [down payment
> or deposit] of our inheritance until the redemption of
> the purchased possession, unto the praise of his glory.
> Ephesians 1:13-14

The "Church" is not a building per se. The Church consists
of all true believers. Believers do not worship the building;

rather they worship the Lord God in heaven. The Lord Jesus Christ purchased the Church with His blood. Paul the apostle advised the elders of the Church:

> Take heed therefore unto yourselves, and to all the flock [the local assembly], over the which the Holy Ghost hath made you overseers, to feed [shepherd] the church of God, which he hath purchased with his own blood.
> Acts 20:28

Paul is ordering the elders to *feed* the believers with God's Word from the Bible in order for them to grow in their walk with the Lord while never forgetting how they were saved.

> [Father God] [13]Who hath delivered us from the power of darkness, and hath translated [transferred] *us* into the kingdom of his dear Son; [14]In whom we have redemption through his blood, *even* the forgiveness of sins.
> Colossians 1:13-14

Everyone has most likely heard of the Ten Commandments which are listed in Exodus chapter 20 and repeated in Deuteronomy chapter 5. God tells us in the very first Commandment that we are not to have any God other than Him. In the verse which precedes this first Commandment God is quoted as He reminds the Israelites of their redemption:

> I *am* the LORD thy God, which brought thee out of the land of Egypt, from the house of bondage.
> Deuteronomy 5:6

Our God reminds us in the last verse of the fourth Commandment that He expects the Israelites to *remember* what He has done for them:

> "And remember that thou wast a servant in the land of Egypt, and *that* the LORD thy God brought thee out thence through a mighty hand and by a stretched out

arm: therefore the LORD thy God commanded thee to keep the sabbath day. Deuteronomy 5:15

For Christian believers today, the Lord Jesus Christ gives us the reminder to *remember* our redemption. When we conduct the part of the worship service called "breaking of the bread" (also called communion) we are remembering that the Savior not only led us out by *a stretched out arm*, but by both arms outstretched, nailed to the cross:

> [19]And he [Jesus] took bread, and gave thanks, and brake *it*, and gave unto them, saying, This is my body which is given for you: this do in remembrance of me. [20]Likewise also the cup after supper, saying, This cup *is* the new testament in my blood, which is shed for you.
> Luke 22:19-20

Paul the apostle further expounds on the importance of *remembering* in his letter to the Corinthians:

> The cup of blessing which we bless, is it not the communion [fellowship] of the blood of Christ? The bread which we break, is it not the communion of the body of Christ? 1 Corinthians 10:16

> For as often as ye eat this bread, and drink *this* cup, ye do show the Lord's death till he come.
> 1 Corinthians 11:26

When two people are separated from each other by reason of disagreement, they are brought back together by understanding—by knowing each other and for the one who is guilty to sincerely ask to be forgiven. When the forgiveness takes place, they are reconciled—they come together again—back into union with one another. Redemption has taken place. Their relationship is restored—their bond is reconciled.

[18]And all things *are* of God, who hath reconciled us to himself by Jesus Christ, and hath given to us the minis-try of reconciliation; [19]To wit [That is], that God was in Christ, reconciling the world unto himself, not imputing their trespasses unto them; and hath committed unto us the word of reconciliation. 2 Corinthians 5:18-19

[21]And you, that were sometime alienated and enemies in *your* mind by wicked works, yet now that he reconciled [22]In the body of his flesh through death, to present you holy and unblamable and unreprovable in his [God's] sight. Colossians 1:21-22

The person who does the forgiving is called the *redeemer.* When this reconciliation occurs in the relationship of man with God, the Lord Jesus Christ is the Redeemer.

[6]To the praise of the glory of his grace, wherein he hath made us accepted in the beloved. [7]In whom we have redemption through his blood, the forgiveness of sins, according to the riches of his grace; [8]Wherein he hath abounded toward us in all wisdom and prudence [understanding, discernment]; Ephesians 1:6-8

Little children [Believers are the adopted children of God and brothers and sisters of Jesus Christ], let no man deceive you: he that doeth [he who *practices*] righteous-ness is righteous [in God's view], even as he [as God] is righteous. 1 John 3:7

Believers are described as God's adopted children in Romans 8:15:

For ye have not received the spirit of bondage [slavery to sin] again to fear; but ye have received the Spirit of adoption, whereby we cry, Abba [Aramaic name for our

intimate relationship with God our Father], Father.
Romans 8:15

The Lord Jesus calls His believing followers His brothers and sisters in Hebrews 2:11:

> For both he that sanctifieth [sanctifies, or *sets apart* believers from the world] and they who are sanctified *are* all of one: for which cause he [Jesus] is not ashamed to call them brethren [His adopted brothers and sisters who all believe in Him]. Hebrews 2:11

Enhanced Discernment

Although spiritual discernment is mainly important because of its *eternal* value, there are other times in this world when we need to use good judgment and reasoning ability to make the best decisions in order to please our God

> But to do good and to communicate [share] forget not: for with such sacrifices God is well pleased.
> Hebrews 13:16

As mentioned previously, believers possess different degrees of discernment. The simplicity of the saving Gospel message and the quest for increased knowledge of God was given in chapter one. In order to better and better understand the Scriptures, one must delve deep to obtain God's intentions more thoroughly. None of us will be able to completely know the mind of Almighty God, but we hunger and thirst for more:

> [34]FOR WHO HATH KNOWN THE MIND OF THE LORD? OR WHO HATH BEEN HIS COUNSELFOR? [35]OR WHO HATH FIRST GIVEN TO HIM, AND IT SHALL BE REC-OMPENSED [repaid] UNTO HIM AGAIN? [36]For of him, and through him, and to him, *are* all things: to whom *be* glory for ever. Amen. Romans 11:34-36

[22]Behold, God exalteth by his power: who teacheth like him? ...
[26]Behold, God is great, and we know *him* not, neither can the number of his years be searched out.
Job 36:22, 26

Who hath directed the Spirit of the LORD, or *being* his counselor hath taught him? Isaiah 40:13

For who hath stood in the counsel of the LORD, and hath perceived and heard his word? who hath marked his word, and heard *it*? Jeremiah 23:18

Granted, in some of Scripture, it is difficult to determine what God is saying to us. It is obvious from knowing *about* Almighty God's power we cannot know all that He knows, but we can continue to try to know more of what He desires of us to please Him. As we mature in His Word, we desire to inquire into the meanings of the words, verses or passages we do not quickly and fully understand.

The Three Ordinances of the New Testament

In the New Testament there are three *traditions*, or *ordinances* prescribed for all the churches to observe:

1. Water baptism to identify ourselves as followers of the Lord Jesus;
2. The Lord's Supper to remember the Lord Jesus' saving work on the cross;
3. Covering or not covering our heads to give glory to the Lord Jesus when we pray or have teaching from God's Word.

In only four verses prior to God's reasoning for the head covering passage, we are told to always glorify our God:

> Whether therefore ye eat, or drink, or whatsoever ye do, do all to the glory of God. 1 Corinthians 10:31

None of the three ordinances are really burdensome, and of the three, the head covering instruction is the least *troublesome*. However, the headship passage is also the most neglected by most churches. It seems odd this would be so, since we consider it is actually a privilege to give glory to God.

One of the most likely reasons the head covering tradition is not being rightly observed is because the Greek interpretation of the English word *covering* has a different translation in the different places where it is used in the passage. Since the glory of God is of utmost importance, this topic calls for clarification.

The example of the head covering tradition is in 1 Corinthians 11:2-15, but we will break after verse five to give explanation before proceeding to verses six to fifteen:

> [2]Now I praise you, brethren [believers; brothers and sisters in Christ], that ye remember me in all things, and keep the ordinances [traditions], as I delivered *them* to you. [3]But I would have you know, that the head of every man is Christ; and the head of the woman *is* the man; and the head of Christ *is* God [the Father]. [To understand this passage, it must be recognized that this verse is telling us that Christ is the glory of His Head, the Father who sent Him; man is the glory of Jesus who produced (created) him; and woman is the glory of man from whom a rib bone was taken to be used to create her. So, what is the glory of the woman? It is her hair which her body produces.] [4]Every man praying or prophesying, having *his* head covered, dishonoreth

his head [This verse gives the very reason we see men take off their hats or caps when involved with prayer or teaching. In this way they do not veil the glory of Christ]. [5]But every woman that prayeth or prophesieth with *her* head uncovered dishonoreth her head: for that is even all one [one and the same] as if she were shaven. 1 Corinthians 11:2-5

We pause the passage here to explain the Greek original meaning for the word *uncovered* in verse five. In Greek the word is *akatakaluptos*. Without the letter *a* prefix, it becomes *katakaluptos* which means to some extent *permanently* covered. With the *a* prefix it becomes somewhat *permanently uncovered*; in other words: shaved, or bald. When we come to verse 15, we will see that there is the entirely different Greek word, *peribolaion*, which refers to a covering which is a *temporary* cover—like a raincoat—or in old English: a *mantle*, something that can be rather quickly put on or taken off. Keeping that in mind, let's continue the passage:

[6]For if the woman be not covered, let her also be shorn [head shaved]: but if it be a shame for a woman to be shorn or shaven, let her be covered [Let her put a temporary cover over her hair so as not to be considered to be the same as being bald and for her to not be ashamed.]. [7]For a man indeed ought not to cover *his* head [Christ is the head of man,; therefore the man needs to display Christ's glory by not covering Christ's glory], forasmuch as he is the image and glory of God: but the woman is the glory of the man [If the woman exposes her hair, she is giving glory to man—not to God.]. [8]For the man is not of the woman; but the woman of the man [from man's rib]. [9]Neither was the man created for the woman; but the woman for the man.

Genesis 2:18, 22: [18]And the LORD God said, *It is* not good that the man should be alone; I will make him a help meet [helper comparable to him] for him. ... [22]And the rib, which the LORD God had taken from man, made he a woman, and brought her unto the man.

Genesis 3:16a, c: [16a]Unto the woman he [God] said ... [16c]thy desire *shall be* to thy husband, and he shall rule over thee.

[10]For this cause ought the woman to have power [a symbol of authority; a cover over her hair, submitting to the divine order] on *her* head because of the angels. [11]Nevertheless neither is the man without [independent of] the woman, neither the woman without the man, in the Lord. [The woman should be submissive just as the angels are submissive to the Lord.] [12]For as the woman *is* of the man, even so *is* the man also by the woman [Here procreation is taken into consideration.]; but all things are of God. [13]Judge in [for] yourselves: is it comely [proper] that a woman pray unto God uncovered [either with her hair exposed or else to be completely baldheaded]? [14]Doth not even nature itself teach you, that, if a man have long hair, it is a shame [dishonor] unto him? [*him* here, could be to the man himself, or, in context, this could also possibly be referring to Christ.] [The next verse, the last of this passage, tells us that a woman covers her hair, because if she does not cover it, she would be dishonoring her head—according to what we read in verse 5: *every woman that prayeth or prophesieth with her head uncovered dishonoreth her head.*] [15]But if a woman have long hair, it is a **glory to** her: for *her* hair is given her for a covering [to keep her from being baldheaded/ashamed.

We read in verse 6: *For if the woman be not covered, let her also be shorn: but if it be a shame for a woman to be shorn or shaven, let her be covered.* A multitude of Bible scholars have taught that verse 15 nullifies all prior verses in the passage. We believe the Holy Spirit would not have wasted His nor our time with those verses if God did not intend for it to be in the Bible (2 Timothy 3:16).] 1 Corinthians 11:6-15

There are many churches today that teach the above passage was only applicable to the believers in Corinth. The question comes up then, "Why is it in my Bible?" Others teach that the *shaved heads* on the women in Corinth was the driving force of this passage due to their immoral *culture* at the time of this writing. However, cultures have never changed God's Word; rather God changes cultures. God tells us that He does not change and His Word does not change:

For I *am* the LORD, I change not. Malachi 3:6a

The grass withereth, the flower fadeth: but the word of our God shall stand for ever. Isaiah 40:8

BUT THE WORD OF THE LORD ENDURETH FOR EVER. And this is the word which by the gospel is preached unto you. 1 Peter 1:25 (Isaiah 40:8)

Craving for Questions to be Answered

As a person grows in his walk with the Lord, spiritual questions arise which call for discernment. For example, "How did I get separated from God to begin with?"

But your iniquities [offenses, sins] have separated between you and your God, and your sins have hid *his* face from you, that he will not hear. Isaiah 59:2

At the moment a new human being is conceived in the mother's womb, the embryo, then the fetus, and eventually the new-born baby—at any of these stages the new one is completely sinless—totally innocent. As a baby becomes a toddler, then a child, a teen, an adult, and finally a senior, a noteworthy change occurs: At some point in the progression (most likely in late childhood or teen years), people become aware of the fact that they have told a lie, used God's name in vain, or looked upon another with lust (even in thoughts), or taken something that did not belong to them, or said they *hate* someone. That sentence just listed five of the Ten Commandments.

Jesus is quoted from *The Sermon on the Mount*:

[21]Ye have heard that it was said by [to] them of old time, THOU SHALT NOT KILL [murder]; and whosoever shall kill [murder] shall be in danger of the judgment: [22a]But I say unto you, That whosoever is angry with his brother without a cause shall be in danger of the judgment. Matthew 5:21-22a

The Spirit of God inspired John the apostle to write:

Whosoever hateth his brother is a murderer: and ye know that no murderer hath eternal life abiding in him. 1 John 3:15

A person who intentionally takes the human life of anyone —including himself—is a murderer. Suicide does not provide a path of escape. Instead it leads one directly to eternal suffering in the Lake of Fire.

Jesus also said:

[27]Ye have heard that it was said by them of old time, THOU SHALT NOT COMMIT ADULTERY. [28]But I say unto you, That whosoever looketh on a woman to lust after her hath committed adultery with her already in his heart. Matthew 5:27-28

If a man even looks with lust at a woman in a pornographic picture or movie, he is committing adultery in his heart.

[8]If we say that we have no sin, we deceive ourselves, and the truth is not in us. [9]If we confess our sins, he is faithful and just to forgive us *our* sins, and to cleanse us from all unrighteousness. [10]If we say that we have not sinned, we make him [God] a liar, and his word is not in us.

1 John 1:8-10

Quoting Warren Henderson in his book: *Mind Frames: Where life's battle is won or lost*:

"If the believer is going to expose his mind to violence, pornography, filthy language, course jesting, and extravagant indulgences, the heart will readily be conformed into a stagnant cesspool of carnal ambitions. *'For as he thinketh in his heart, so is he'* (Prov. 23:7). Physically you are what you eat, but spiritually you become what you think upon. It is simply the sowing and reaping principles of the harvest. The three laws of the harvest are: (1) you reap what you sow; (2) you reap more than what you sow; and (3) you reap later than you sow. Paul explains that if *'a man soweth to his flesh, he shall of the flesh reap corruption'* (see Gal. 6:7-8). When a believer feeds on (thinks upon) what is corrupt, it must lead to a legitimate harvest of corruption. It will be realized long after the initial seeds were sown that the repercussions were far more devastating than what could have ever been imagined. The nude images that a young man tucks away in his mind will be used by Satan to stir up dissatisfaction with his own wife for many years to come. So why hurt yourself, your wife, your family, and your God? The harvest of pain is just not worth it.

> Flee also youthful lusts: but follow righteous-
> ness, faith, charity [love], peace, with them that
> call on the Lord out of a pure heart.
> 2 Timothy 2:22

The overall diet of the believer's mind boils down to proper thinking and reasoning. Regarding appropriate discernment, Paul writes the following:

> [19]For your obedience is come abroad unto all *men*.
> I am glad therefore on your behalf: but yet I would
> have you wise unto that which is good, and sim-
> ple concerning evil. [20]And the God of peace shall
> bruise Satan under your feet shortly. The grace of
> our Lord Jesus Christ be with you. Amen.
> Romans 16:19-20

The child of God is to discern between what is holy and what is evil, what is wise and what is foolish. What is holy and wise should be obeyed, and what is evil and foolish should be shunned. The matter of discerning between right and wrong behavior is dependent upon knowing the commandments of Scripture. Discerning what is wise and what is foolish is dependent upon knowing God's commandments, warnings, principles, promises, and the lessons learned from personal narratives in Scripture. In fact, the Lord addressed the matter of being wise and not foolish much more often than the matter of what is right and what is wrong, though the latter would be included in what is wise and foolish. Gaining discernment of what is wise and what is foolish requires prayer, study, godly counsel, and the leading of the Holy Spirit in our lives."[21]

It is downright, out-and-out serious to call our Creator and Savior of life a *liar* and to not remember that He is also our righteous Judge—this is bold and blatantly, eternally dangerous. The reason men are afraid to die is because of this eternal fact: It is a sad situation if a man goes to his grave without God's forgiveness.

> [20b]for by the law [Ten Commandments] *is* the knowledge of sin. [21a]But now the righteousness of God;
>
> [22]Even the righteousness of God *which is* by faith of Jesus Christ unto all and upon all them that believe: for there is no difference; [23]For all have sinned, and come short of the glory of God. Romans 3:20b-21a, 22-23

In *God's view*, believers *practice* righteousness simply because they truly believe in God. And God accepts only the righteous into His kingdom. Of course, because of Adam's DNA indwelling him, the believer still occasionally sins—even in his thoughts— but the indwelling Spirit overcomes the evil and prompts the believer to quickly recognize his sin and to sincerely ask forgiveness. Upon doing so, the Spirit clears the believer's conscience and his heart is clean.

Everyone, upon reaching the age of accountability, with the exception of the Lord Jesus Christ, has broken at least one of these Ten Commandments. And in doing so, God separates them from Himself, because God does not accept sin. Period.

The baby is *home free*. But the accountable person is condemned. The punishment for that guilt is so grueling that it lasts for ever and ever.

Jesus is quoted:

> He that believeth on him is not condemned: but he that believeth not is condemned already because he hath not believed in the name of the only begotten Son of God. John 3:18

That verse addresses the fact that unbelieving people are fearful of dying—because those who do not believe will eventually go to eternal suffering in the never quenchable Lake of Fire. Jesus is again quoted:

> [42]And whosoever shall offend [cause to stumble] one of *these* little ones that believe in me, it is better for him that a millstone were hanged about his neck, and he were cast into the sea. [43]And if thy hand offend thee [if your flesh makes you sin], cut it off: it is better for thee to enter into life maimed, than having two hands to go into hell, into the fire that never shall be quenched: [44]Where THEIR WORM DIETH NOT, AND THE FIRE IS NOT QUENCHED [Capitalized because it is quoting Isaiah 66:24; Jeremiah 7:20]. [45]And if thy foot, offend thee [makes you sin], cut it off: it is better for thee to enter halt [lame] into life, than having two feet to be cast into hell, into the fire that never shall be quenched: [46]Where THEIR WORM DIETH NOT, AND THE FIRE IS NOT QUENCHED. [47]And if thine eye offend thee, pluck it out: it is better for thee to enter into the kingdom of God with one eye, than having two eyes to be cast into hell fire; [48]WHERE THEIR WORM DIETH NOT, AND THE FIRE IS NOT QUENCHED. Mark 9:42-48

But the good news is the Gospel message: Jesus Christ took the most unimaginable, cruel punishment for everyone who repents of their sins and believes in the one true God: The Father, Son, and Holy Spirit. Jesus shed His blood to forgive and died on the cross so that believers could be saved from the second death—the Lake of Fire. Jesus was raised from the dead, ascended to heaven, is still alive, and God *promises* to send Him back to the clouds to have believers meet Him in the air and then on to everlasting life with Him. God has never told a lie. God always keeps His promises:

> [1b]the acknowledging of the truth which is after [according to] godliness; [2]In [every true believer's] hope of eternal life, which God, that [who] cannot lie, promised before the world began; Titus 1:1b-2

> And God hath both raised up the Lord, and will also raise up us by his own power. 1 Corinthians 6:14

> Knowing that he which raised up the Lord Jesus shall raise up us also by Jesus, and shall present *us* [the twelve apostles] with you. 2 Corinthians 4:14

> But if the Spirit of him that raised up Jesus from the dead dwell in you, he that raised up Christ from the dead shall also quicken [give life to] your mortal bodies by his Spirit that dwelleth in you. Romans 8:11

Upon the repenting, confessing, and believing, God sees the person as no longer being a sinner, but in His view He sees us as being righteous—*innocent*—*with the righteousness of God Himself*. So God redeems the new believer back to no longer being separated from Himself, and accepts him into fellowship with His Son.

What Happened to Those Innocent Young Ones?

> [2]And Jesus called a little child unto him, and set him in the midst of them, [3]And said, Verily I say unto you, Except ye be converted, and become as little children, ye shall not enter into the kingdom of heaven. Matthew 18:2-3

But Jesus said, Suffer [Allow] little children, and forbid them not, to come unto me: for of such [*innocent* ones] is the kingdom of heaven. Matthew 19:14

But when Jesus saw *it*, he was much displeased, and said unto them, Suffer the little children to come unto me, and forbid them not: for of such is the kingdom of God. Mark 10:14

[16]But Jesus called them *unto him*, and said, Suffer little children to come unto me, and forbid them not: for of such is the kingdom of God. [17]Verily I say unto you, Whosoever shall not receive the kingdom of God as a little child [as a righteous—innocent person] shall in no wise enter therein. Luke 18:16-17

But your little ones, which ye said should be a prey [victims], them will I bring in, and they shall know the land which ye have despised. Numbers 14:31

Moreover your little ones, which ye said should be a prey, and your children, which in that day had no knowledge between good and evil, they shall go in thither, and unto them will I give it, and they shall possess it. Deuteronomy 1:39

But saith the LORD, Even the captives of the mighty shall be taken away, and the prey of the terrible shall be delivered: for I will contend with him that contendeth with thee, and I will save thy children. Isaiah 49:25

God sees us as not being guilty when He knows we believe in Him. God's truth tells us that the innocent will be saved.

The great majority of parents love their children so much that they fervently desire to see them forever. The longest word in the English language is *eternity*. That greatest possible length of time is what loving fathers, mothers, and grandparents want for being with their little ones.

When Should a Child be Taught Discernment?

Train up a child in the way he should go: and when he is old, he will not depart from it. Proverbs 22:6

[13]Withhold not correction from the child: for *if* thou beatest him with a rod, he shall not die. [14]Thou shall beat him with the rod, and shalt deliver his soul from hell. Proverbs 23:13-14

"*It does not take a village* to develop discernment for children. Raising a child to make the best decisions and choices in life calls for genuine, loving parents. The sound doctrine of God's Word is the best counsel parents can be sure of; to trust and to depend upon.

Every child and grandchild, whom we hope to see for all future time, forever in heaven, should be taught what is right and what is wrong early in life.

To give children a good *education* in manners, arts and science, is important; to give them a religious [biblical] *education* is indispensable; and an immense responsibility rests on parents and guardians who neglect these duties.[22]

Proverbs 13:24 prescribes for parents to discipline the child *promptly*. It goes without saying, "Never punish the child out of anger." Abusing a baby, a youngster, or even a teen or adult is not acceptable in society. It is deplorable in the eyes of the Lord. Rather discipline them out of love...let them know the reason for disciplining...and *begin soon*.

Of course, a baby has only his cry to communicate that he is hungry or needs his diaper to be changed. The parent needs to understand the message the infant is conveying. But, when it becomes obvious that the little one is behaving in a wrongful manner, then disciplinary action should begin:

> He that spareth [does not use] his rod hateth [hates] his son: but he that loveth him chasteneth [disciplines] him betimes [early, *promptly*]. Proverbs 13:24

The *rod* in Hebrew literally translates to *a stick for punishing.*[23]

Hateth in Proverbs 13:24 is used comparatively. The parent who does not discipline does not really love his child properly. While the popular adage: "Spare the rod, spoil the child" is not a direct biblical quotation, it certainly expresses a biblical idea.

Love and discipline go together. The *rod* does not necessarily mean a spanking, but simply whatever physical discipline is reasonable for the offense. The rod refers to a branch or switch. It is a small object that stings, but does not inflict serious bodily harm. The use of the rod for spanking is clearly taught in Scripture in preference to spanking with one's hand:[24]

God disciplines His own children. His only begotten Child was the Lord Jesus Christ. He gave Jesus to all mankind by sacrificing Him to take the disciplinary judgment for all who have offended God. The Father also considers all believers to be His adopted children, so He, when necessary, disciplines those who believe in Him as well:

³For consider him [God] that endured such contradiction [hostility] of sinners against himself, lest ye be wearied and faint [discouraged] in your minds [souls]. ... ⁵And ye have forgotten the exhortation which speaketh unto you as unto children [sons and daughters], MY CHILDREN DESPISE NOT THOU THE CHASTENING [discipline] OF THE LORD, NOR FAINT [be discouraged] WHEN THOU [you] ARE REBUKED OF HIM [by the Father]: ⁶FOR WHOM THE LORD LOVETH HE CHASTENETH, AND SCOURGETH EVERY SON WHOM HE RECEIVETH. [Capitalized words quoted from Proverbs 3:11-12] ⁷If ye endure chastening, God dealeth with you as with sons; for what son is he whom the father chasteneth not? ... ⁹Furthermore we have had fathers of our flesh which corrected *us*, and we gave *them* reverence: shall we not much rather be in subjection unto the Father of spirits, and live? ¹⁰For they verily [truly] for a few days chastened *us* after their own pleasure [as seemed best to them]; but he [God] for *our* profit, that *we* might be partakers of his holiness [The Father views us as being holy and righteous when we believe in God.]. ¹¹Now no chastening [discipline] for the present seemeth to be joyous, but grievous: nevertheless afterward it yieldeth [results in] the peaceable fruit of righteousness unto them which are exercised thereby.
Hebrews 12:3, 5-7, 9-11

For whom the LORD loveth he correcteth; even as a father the son *in whom* he delighteth. Proverbs 3:12

The disciplining we, the whole world, deserved was laid upon the Son of God. When you genuinely, tearfully understand that the chastisement was for you—when you believe—then the Holy Spirit within you will cause you to appreciate, love and obey the Lord Jesus. The Lord gave Isaiah the vision to tell how God would substitute and punish Jesus for us and for our sins:

> But he *was* wounded for our transgressions [blatant sins], *he was* bruised for our iniquities [sins]: the chastisement of our peace *was* upon him; and with his stripes [from being scourged ((Matthew 27:26; Mark 15:15; John 19:1)] we are healed [healed of our sin condition (Romans 3:25)]. Isaiah 53:5

Ramifications

A patriotic father of two sons desired to share what he'd learned from his own mistakes. In his beloved homeland, the absolute disrespect for authority which has emerged in the last fifty years in homes, schools, communities, and society in general, inspired the father to relate this story:

In the 1960's and 70's public rulings related to teachings on how to develop discernment were being *revolutionized*. Thirty to fifty years later, from 2000 to 2020, the results of those changes were being sorely revealed. What should have been peaceable protests turned out to be extreme rioting, looting, murdering, burning of private businesses, and hatred for law enforcement.

Both sons of the dad mentioned, being born in the early and mid 1970's, were disciplined with the switch, but during the space of time between their ages, society called it a crime of *child abuse* if a youngster got a *spanking*. In regards to *respect of authority*, the two sons, nearly four years of age apart, turned out to have totally different attitudes. This father loved and still loves both sons dearly and equally. The father would eventually gain a clear understanding of the deception brought on by *man*—the so-called *experts*.

Having been intimidated by possible *child abuse* accusations, the father had turned to giving the younger son much more *disciplining* by man's methods of *grounding, time outs,* or *standing in the corner*—as if this would be *better* for him than a spanking. However, while standing in the corner the younger son was then deprived of the parental attention he would otherwise have received—had he not been required to spend so much *time alone.* The consequence of the modern ways came to vivid reality about the time the younger became a man and would end up getting into trouble with employers and eventually with the law—mainly for *disrespecting authority.*

During the time a child is left to himself, his mind can wander to the point of even entertaining himself. On the other hand, the little sting on his buttocks does not result in death nor permanent disability. Rather it produces negative motivation to think about not repeating the offense. And soon afterwards, loving companionship with the parents returns. Moreover, later in life, the God inspired upbringing results in an enormous magnitude of respect for those parents who gave attention and showed loving care.

When a child is *grounded* or *standing in the corner*, one must wonder what it is he is thinking about: is he fuming about how he's lost the basic God-given-right of freedom? Or is he concentrating for long periods of time upon how much he dislikes—or even *hates*—his unkind, uncaring parents? No wonder he can build up such a resistance to authority.

The moral of the story is to listen to God: discipline with the rod (stick) and do it *promptly* with reason of love (Proverbs 13:24).

It is vitally important to have development for success in life with sound doctrine by *education* versus *indoctrination* by society. It *does not* take a *village* to raise a child. *It takes parents grounded in God's Word to raise a child*—mature loving parents well versed in God's ways—not man's ways. Society restrains the disciplinary actions necessary for developing good judgment and reasoning ability. God provides a lighted path to eternal life by giving sound advice for listening to Him on how to develop the discernment and stay on the right path. Choosing the right way requires one to have discernment—the ability to make the best choices in every decision and action.

The father in this story is the author you are reading.

Of course the father spoken of here is not without blame. In fact, he is ashamed of his own sinful, wretched past. He realizes his own shortcomings, and he knows his sons are also aware of their dad's mistakes. Dad only prays that that both young men would learn from their own, and their dad's, errors. The dad now is eternally grateful for having received the grace of God to have this life-changing relationship with the Lord Jesus Christ and prays to have precious unity with his cherished, beloved sons.

> "The soul who sins shall die. The son shall not bear the guilt of the father, nor the father bear the guilt of the son. The righteousness of the righteous shall be upon himself, and the wickedness of the wicked shall be upon himself." Ezekiel 18:20 NKJV

> For all have sinned, and come short of the glory of God. Romans 3:23

> But God commendeth his [demonstrates His own] love toward us, in that, while we were yet sinners, Christ died for us. Romans 5:8

> In the lips of him that hath understanding wisdom is found: but a rod *is* for the back of him that is void of understanding. Proverbs 10:13

A whip for the horse, a bridle for the ass [donkey], and a rod for the fool's back. Proverbs 26:3

Foolishness *is* bound in the heart of a child; *but* the rod of correction shall drive it [foolishness] far from him. Proverbs 22:15

Bodily punishment is required for youngsters because they have no other way of learning and knowing right from wrong. They are born naturally unaware that they are foolish.

[14]Thou shalt beat him with the rod, and shalt deliver his soul from hell. [15]My son, if thine heart be wise, my heart shall rejoice, even mine. Proverbs 23:14-15

The rod and reproof [conviction] give wisdom: but a child left *to himself* bringeth his mother to shame. Proverbs 29:15

No loving father or mother would want their child to be called a fool and see them put to shame. It is unsurprisingly ingrained in parents to desire for their offspring to succeed. Graduations, weddings, careers, and most importantly: *eternal* salvation; are all goals of loving parents. It's difficult to imagine anyone wanting to see their kids called fools. (The KJV has all first words of each chapter capitalized):

THE proverbs of Solomon. A wise son maketh a glad father: but a foolish son *is* the heaviness [grief] of his mother. Proverbs 10:1

It is as sport to a fool to do mischief: but a man of understanding hath wisdom. Proverbs 10:23

A fool despiseth his father's instruction: but he that regardeth reproof [conviction] is prudent. Proverbs 15:5

He that begetteth [He who conceives] a fool [scoffer] *doeth it* to his sorrow: and the father of a fool hath no joy. Proverbs 17:21

Speak not in the ears of a fool: for he will despise the wisdom of thy words. Proverbs 23:9

AS snow in summer, and as rain in harvest, so honor is not seemly [fitting] for a fool. Proverbs 26:1

Credit for writing the Book of Proverbs is given by most biblical scholars to Solomon, a son of King David. Solomon Prayed for wisdom and discernment:

[9]Give therefore thy servant an understanding heart to judge thy people, that I may discern between good and bad: for who is able to judge this thy so great a people? [10]And the speech pleased the Lord, that Solomon had asked this thing. [11]And God said unto him, Because thou hast asked this thing, and hast not asked for thyself long life; neither hast asked riches for thyself, nor hast asked the life of thine enemies; but hast asked for thyself understanding to discern judgment; Behold, I have done according to thy words: lo, I have given thee a wise and an understanding heart; so that there was none like thee before thee, neither after thee shall any arise like unto thee. 1 Kings 3:9-12

Proverbs is jam-packed with words of wisdom. It consists of 31 short chapters. If parents would read to their children, one chapter a day—which would take only about ten to fifteen minutes—the entire Book could be read in one month. The recommended time that the parents and child should read this Book together is as soon as a child is old enough to understand and knows he is going to be accountable to God for his behavior.

The enormous value of sharing God's wisdom which was imputed upon Solomon cannot be over stated. Not only is discernment to be gained by doing so, but also *wisdom*. In fact, it just might be the amount of wisdom needed to inspire one to read God's entire Word—the Word which saves and guides one to eternal life:

> For I am not ashamed of the gospel of Christ; for it [the Gospel message] is the power of God unto salvation.
> Romans 1:16a

The two words, *gospel* and *salvation* beg definition: "the Gospel words are the *saving instrument.*"[25]

First: The Gospel Message

The Gospel message is translated to mean *the good news*. It is not lengthy. This short message consists of four main points:

1. Jesus Christ shed His blood to forgive us of our sins and *died* in our place.
2. He was buried inside a closed tomb and was raised from the dead on the third day.
3. He was seen alive for forty days before being seen ascending through a cloud.
4. He promises to return to the air to take us up; thereby saving us before the wrath.

Paul the apostle writes:

> [3]For I delivered unto you first of all that which I also received, how that Christ died for our sins according to the scriptures [prophecies]. [4]And that he was buried, and that he rose again the third day according to the scriptures [prophecies]: [5]And that he was seen of Cephas [Peter], then of the twelve. [6a]After that he was seen of above [by more than] five hundred brethren at once; 1 Corinthians 15:3-6a

Luke, the Gentile physician, writes:

> [The apostles] [3]to whom also he [Jesus] showed himself alive after his passion [suffering] by many infallible proofs, being seen of them forty days, and speaking of the things pertaining to the kingdom of God. ... [9]And when he had spoken these things, while they beheld, he was taken up; and a cloud received him out of their sight. Acts 1:3, 9

In the Gospel According to Mark, he writes:

> So then after the Lord had spoken unto them, he was received up into heaven, and sat on the right hand of God. Mark 16:19

> And if I go and prepare a place for you, I will come again, and receive you unto myself; that where I am, *there* ye may be also. John 14:3

Those four points, Christ's witnessed death, burial, resurrection, witnessed ascension, and His promise to return for us, are the essence of the Gospel message.

What is Salvation?

> For I am not ashamed of the gospel of Christ: for it is the power of God unto salvation to every one that believeth; to the Jew first, and also to the Greek.
> Romans 1:16

The word *salvation* as it is translated from the original Greek *soteria*, in Romans 1:16, means

> "the spiritual and eternal deliverance granted immediately by God to those who accept His conditions of repentance and faith in the Lord Jesus, to whom alone it is to be obtained, and upon confession of Him as Lord; for this purpose the gospel is the saving instrument of the present [moment] experience of God's power to deliver from the bondage of sin."[26]

In short, *salvation* means *saved from God's punishment*: the second death *in the lake of fire for our offenses against His Law*; and saved to a *restored eternal life with our sinless Lord in heaven*.

Salvation can be compared to a wrecked car from the salvage yard being brought out to be *restored*. Likewise, the sinner's soul can be restored upon repentance and belief in the Savior. This is also called a *regenerated* soul, or a *redeemed* life.

If a married couple becomes separated, and then they come together again, it can be said they have been *reconciled*. Their relationship with each other has been *salvaged*. A believer—restored person—has a salvaged relationship with God. Since the person had offended God, because of his sin, God had then separated him from Himself. Until repentance—that is, forgiveness has been sincerely requested by the sinning person.

Without being sincerely remorseful and repenting, he would remain separated. Other words for this *salvation* are *redemption* and *atonement*. Upon being redeemed we are made to be *at one* with God again. Our souls have been salvaged—renewed, restored, redeemed, rescued.

The holy nature of God and the sinful nature of man are the two factors which lead to God separating all sin from Himself.

"The Hebrew word translated *holiness* comes from a root meaning *to separate* or *cut off*. The primary meaning of *holiness* implies God's positive quality of self-affirming purity; the secondary meaning implies separation, particularly separation from sin. The holiness of God means He is absolutely pure and absolutely separate from (and above) all His creatures, and also separate from sin and evil. **Illustration:** Because God is holy, all sin is offensive to Him. For this reason He had to break fellowship with His own Son when Jesus became our sin-bearer:"[27]

And about the ninth hour [the sixth hour of Jesus being nailed to the cross] Jesus cried with a loud voice, *'Eli, Eli, lama sabachthani?* That is to say, My GOD, MY GOD, WHY HAST THOU FORSAKEN ME? Matthew 27:46

For he hath made him *to be* sin for us, who knew no sin; that we might be made the righteousness of God in him. 2 Corinthians 5:21

"Only through the identification of Christ with our sin as our sacrifice can we be reconciled to God. **Application:** When the Scriptures mention the holiness of God, they also stress the personal holiness of His people."[28]

[3]And God said, Let there be light: and there was light. [4]And God saw the light, that *it was* good: and God divided the light from the darkness. Genesis 1:3-4

Ye are all the children [believers who are sons and daughters] of light, and the children of the day: we are not of the night, nor of darkness. 1 Thessalonians 5:5

The Lord Jesus, being that *Light*, is quoted:

[19]And this is the condemnation, that light [the light] has come into the world, and men loved darkness rather than light, because their deeds were evil. [20]For every one that doeth [practices] evil hateth the light, lest his deeds should be reproved [exposed]. [21]But he that doeth truth cometh to the light, that his deeds may be made manifest, that they are wrought in [their good deeds are being done due to the indwelling Holy Spirit of] God. John 3:19-21

The forgiveness is based entirely upon the shed blood of Jesus Christ—the shed blood that a person believes in to obtain the salvation for eternal life in the kingdom of God.

How much more shall the blood of Christ [instead of the *temporary* forgiveness from blood of animals], who through the eternal Spirit offered himself without spot [without blemish, with no sin in Him] to God, purge [cleanse] your conscience from dead works to serve the living God? Hebrews 9:14

Neither is there salvation in any other: for there is none other name [than Jesus Christ of Nazareth (v. 10)] under heaven given among men, whereby we must be saved. Acts 4:12

For the life of the flesh *is* in the blood: and I have given it to you upon the altar to make an atonement for your souls: for it *is* the blood *that* maketh an atonement for the soul. Leviticus 17:11

Of course "if any animal, including a human being, loses its blood, it dies. Its blood therefore, gives it life. The shed blood of Jesus Christ gives visible evidence that life had indeed been offered up by the Father's sacrifice of His only begotten Son."[29]

And almost all things are by the law purged [cleansed] with blood; and without shedding of blood is no remission [forgiveness]. Hebrews 9:22

[8b]THE WORD IS NIGH [near] THEE, *EVEN* IN THY MOUTH, AND IN THY HEART: that is, the word of faith, which we preach; [9]That if thou shalt confess with thy mouth the Lord Jesus, and shalt believe in thine heart that God hath raised him from the dead, thou shalt be saved. [10]For with the heart man believeth unto righteousness; and with the mouth confession is made unto salvation. [11]For the scripture saith, WHOEVER BELIEVETH ON HIM SHALL NOT BE ASHAMED.
Romans 10:8b-11

For *whoever calls on the name of the LORD* shall be saved. Romans 10:13

The salvation we receive for our believing in Jesus Christ our God and Savior is *eternal*—that is, the eternity of our spirits and souls already have eternal life upon the very moment we believe. And immediately after the moment we are saved, nothing can take this away—because it is *eternal*.

[38]For I am persuaded, that neither death, nor life, nor angels, nor principalities, nor powers, nor things

present, nor things to come, [39]Nor height, nor depth, nor any other creature, shall be able to separate us from the love of God, which is in Christ Jesus our Lord. Romans 8:38-39

Jesus, the Shepherd of all believers, is quoted:
[27]My sheep [believers in Jesus] hear my voice, and I know them, and they follow me. [28]And I give unto them eternal life; and they shall never perish, neither shall any *man* pluck them out of my hand. [29]My Father, which gave *them* me, is greater than all; and no *man* is able to pluck *them* out of my Father's hand. [30]I and *my* Father are one. John 10:27-30

When a person becomes fully persuaded and truly believes in the Triune God, Father, Son, and Holy Spirit, and His entire Word, there is *no power* that can halt this person's eternal life.

Out of Time

Time does not end in eternity. But temporary flesh life does end on this earth. Time does not end, it goes on forever...but time can be short.

The day of the Lord so cometh as a thief in the night. 1Thessalonians 5:2b

But this I say, brethren, the time is short. 1 Corinthians 7:29a

behold, now is the accepted time; behold, now is the day of salvation. 2 Corinthians 6:2b

for the time *is* at hand. Revelation 3:3b

for *it is* time so seek the LORD, till he come and rain righteousness upon you. Hosea 10:12b

prepare to meet thy God. Amos 4:12

The Lord Jesus said:
Take ye heed, watch and pray: for ye know not when the time is. Mark 13:33

Every day when we wake up from a night's sleep, we are one day closer to meeting our God. We can take the attitude: "nothing will take my life today." But many have lost their lives instantly in unexpected ways. Some say, "I will wait to ask forgiveness until I finish enjoying the immediate pleasures I am enjoying."

Wherefore, as by one man sin entered into the world, and death by sin; and so death passed upon all men, for that all have sinned. Romans 5:12

And as it is appointed unto men once to die, but after this the judgment. Hebrews 9:27

The Lord Jesus said:
[A certain rich man] [19]said, And I will say to my soul, thou hast much goods laid up for many years; take thine ease, eat, drink, *and* be merry. [20]But God said unto him, *Thou* fool, this night thy soul shall be required of thee: then whose shall those things be, which thou has provided? Luke 12:19-20

Again, Paul, a chosen apostle of the Lord Jesus said:
> behold, now *is* the accepted time; behold, now *is* the
> day of salvation. 2 Corinthians 6:2b

Dear reader, be prepared. Isaiah quotes our Almighty God:
> Look unto me, and be ye saved. Isaiah 45:22a

The Almighty God Lord Jesus Christ is quoted:
> seek and ye shall find; knock, and it shall be opened
> unto you. Luke 11:9b

The Lord Jesus is again quoted:
> Behold, I stand at the door, and knock. Revelation 3:20a

But the one who is curious and not yet persuaded as to
whether or not he believes must realize there are wolves in
sheep's clothing lurking and preying upon his kind.

The Bible tells us over 65 times such phrases as "watch out,"
"be careful," "do not be deceived." False teachers outnumber
those who bring forth only God's truths. We all must consider
the sources of what we read and hear. This *considering* is called
discerning.

All humans, including those who are temporarily alive on
earth, and even those who have, for either long or short time,
been in their graves, will be resurrected from the dead, to meet
the Lord Jesus for things they have done:

Luke quotes Paul the apostle:
> [14b]so worship I the God of my fathers, believing all
> things which are written in the law and in the prophets:
> [15]And have hope toward God, which they themselves
> [Paul's Pharisee accusers] also allow [accept], that there

shall be a resurrection of the dead, both of the just and unjust. Acts 24:14b-15

Paul writes to believers; the people whom Christ will judge in heaven:

> [10b]we [brothers and sisters in Christ (v. 10a)] shall all stand before the judgment seat of Christ. [11]For it is written, AS I LIVE, SAITH THE LORD, EVERY KNEE SHALL BOW TO ME, AND EVERY TONGUE SHALL CONFESS TO GOD. [12]So then every one of us shall give account of himself to God. Romans 14:10b-12

> For we must all appear before the judgment seat of Christ; that every one may receive the things *done* in *his* body, according to that he hath done, whether *it be* good or bad. 2 Corinthians 5:10

Paul reminds that the Lord Jesus will also judge unbelievers on this earth:

> [9]Wherefore God [the Father] also hath highly exalted him [Jesus], and given him a name which is above every name: [10]That at the name of Jesus every knee should bow, of *things* in heaven, and *things* in earth, and *things* under the earth; [11]And *that* every tongue should confess that Jesus Christ *is* Lord, to the glory of God the Father. Philippians 2:9-11

John quotes the Lord Jesus:

> For the Father judgeth no man, but hath committed all judgment unto the Son: John 5:22

^{26}For as the Father hath life in himself; so hath he given to the Son to have life in himself; ^{27}And hath given him authority to execute judgment also, because he is the Son of man. ^{28}Marvel not at this: for the hour is coming, in the which all that are in the graves shall hear his voice, ^{29}And shall come forth; they that have done good, unto the resurrection of life, and they that have done evil, unto the resurrection of damnation. John 5:26-29

^{36}But I say unto you, That every idle word that men shall speak, they shall give account thereof in the day of judgment. ^{37}For by thy words thou shalt be justified, and by thy words thou shalt be condemned.
Matthew 12:36-37

Justice and mercy meet at the cross. Jesus the Judge will reward all according to either the good deeds or the bad:

^{26}For what is a man profited, if he shall gain the whole world, and lose his own soul? or what shall a man give in exchange for his soul? ^{27}For the Son of man [Christ the Judge] shall come in the glory of his Father with his angels; and then he shall reward every man according to his works. Matthew 16:26-27

The next chapter will begin with a warning to remember how important it is to know where the truth comes from.

The Bible, over sixty-five times, gives us warnings such as "Watch out!" "Be careful!" "Do not be deceived."

BLOVED, believe not every spirit, but try the spirits whether they are of God: because many false prophets are gone out into the world. 1 John 4:1

When we seek the truth, should we trust man, or should we trust God who created man? It truly is a matter of life and death.

> For the wages of sin *is* death; but the gift of God *is* eternal life through Jesus Christ our Lord. Romans 6:23

Chapter 5

Relying on the Right Source for Discernment

Should we Trust the created or the Creator?

When supposed *information* is taught, it is crucially essential to know that the stated information is truly from a reliable source. Although repeating what was mentioned in chapter 3, this subject has never been more important that it is today. *Anonymous sources* are probably anonymous for reason of manipulation. God, in His Word, warns us over and again to not be deceived. The press, and both religious and political figures, are notorious for using unidentified informants or "whistle blowers" for pushing a false agenda.

If the subject is history, is the history *original*, or has it been *revised*? Since no mere created being was there when the universe and this world were established, and if the topic is creation, are the scientific methods and experiments really trustworthy?

Even though people attempt to erase history by changing higher schools' curriculums, actual, true history stays forever.

With what in reality came to pass...does not go away...simply because someone does not want to admit that it really happened.

The Scriptures have been scrutinized from the beginning. But the Bible has endured every form of attack and is still alive today.

> [12]For the word of God is quick [living], and powerful, and sharper than any twoedged sword, piercing even to the dividing asunder [division] of soul and spirit, and of the joints and marrow, and *is* a discerner [able to judge] of the thoughts and intents [intentions] of the heart. [13]Neither is there any creature that is not manifest in [not hidden from] his sight [God's sight]: but all things *are* naked and opened unto the eyes of him [God] with whom we have to do [must give an account; an explanation]. Hebrews 4:12-13

It should be noted that the first verse in that passage tells us there are three essential parts to our created beings: spirit, soul, and body. And God's Word has to do with all three.

Our Creator—all Three Beings—is both singular and plural. Beyond our possible comprehension, God exists in Three Persons. Each One is often referred to as being *God*, but to have knowledge of who God is, it is essential to know that all Three must be embraced. Quoting Jabe Nicholson, "The word *time* is comprised of three essential parts. To have *all* of time, all three components must be included: 1) Past, 2) Present, and 3) Future.

"Just as it is necessary for the essence of time to contain all three elements of past, present and future; and for the essence of fire to have all three essential ingredients of ignition, fuel, and air; it is also essential to include all Three Beings to have the genuine essence of God." All Three were already there in the beginning:

> IN the beginning God created the heaven and the earth. Genesis 1:1

This first verse in the Bible already contains the Three essential Persons of God in the meaning of the Name *God*:

> *God* (Heb. Elōhīm): This form of the divine name occurs 2,570 times in the Old Testament. The plural ending *im* indicates a plural of majesty and takes a singular verb.[30]

Moreover, the Third Person is named in verse two, and the First Person in verse three:

> [2]And the earth was without form, and void; and darkness *was* upon the face of the deep. And the Spirit of God moved upon the face of the waters. [3]And God [the Father] said, Let there be light. Genesis 1:2-3

And the Father is quoted in Hebrews chapter one naming the Second Person, His Son, as the Person of God who performed the actual work of creation.

> [8a]But unto the Son *he saith*, ... [10]And, THOU, LORD, IN THE BEGINNING HAST LAID THE FOUNDATION OF THE EARTH; AND THE HEAVENS ARE THE WORKS OF THINE HANDS. Hebrews 1:8a, 10

> THE heavens declare the glory of God; and the firmament showeth his handiwork. Psalm 19:1

> The word *firmament* in Hebrew is *raqiyai* which translates to 1) that which is fixed and steadfast, rather than that which is solid. 1a) The application to the heavenly

bodies is simple and beautiful: 1b) they are not fickle and uncertain in their movements, but are regulated by a law that they cannot pass over. 2) It comes from *raqa* which means spread out. The firmament, then is that which is spread or stretched out—hence expanse. Thus it is extended and fixed, or fixed space. 3) The interplanetary spaces are measured out by God, and though the stars are ever moving, they generally preserve fixed relative positions; their movements are not erratic, not in straight lines, but in orbits, and thus, though ever changing, they are always the same.[31]

Seeing the power and glory of our Savior in creation, one cannot help but take in His loving grace and mercy for laying down His life for those who believe in Him; not forgetting the choices He allows: Either His free offer of salvation or His wrath for those who reject Him. Justice and mercy meet at the cross. The Lord Jesus Christ is the Judge who will either save us or convict us.

Trusting the Creator should come naturally when we consider the magnificence of His Divinely inspired, flawless, inerrant Word.

The Bible is so perfectly put together by the Holy Spirit of God, that it contains splendor not thought possible. The very center chapter of the Bible is Psalm 118. There are 1,188 chapters previous to Psalm 118, and 1,188 subsequent chapters. The preceding chapter, Psalm 117, is the shortest chapter in the entire Bible with only two verses, and the chapter which follows, Psalm 119, is the longest with 176 verses.

Then, verse 118:8 provides this discerning advice: "*It* is better to trust in the LORD than to put confidence in man." Psalm 118:8. We should heed this advice.

This knowledge should give us discernment to question man's ways and to put the Savior in the center of our constant decision making process.

> The way of fools seems right to them, but the wise listen to advice. Proverbs 12:15 NIV

> Be not wise in thine own eyes: fear the LORD, and depart from evil. Proverbs 3:7

> [5]Trust in the LORD with all thine heart; and lean not unto thine own understanding. [6]In all thy ways acknowledge him, and he shall direct thy paths.
> Proverbs 3:5-6

> The wise shall inherit glory: but shame shall be the promotion [the legacy] of fools. Proverbs 3:35

> A wise *man* feareth [reveres God, stands in awe of God], and departeth from evil: but the fool rageth, and is confident [self-confident, not relying on God's advice]. Proverbs 14:16

> Thy word *is* true *from* the beginning: and every one of thy righteous judgments *endureth* for ever.
> Psalm 119:160

> Seest thou a man wise in his own conceit [eyes]? *There is* more hope of a fool than of him. Proverbs 26:12

> He that trusteth in his own heart is a fool: but whoso walketh wisely, he shall be delivered [rescued from danger; escape from danger of sin]. Proverbs 28:26

We definitely do need to rely upon the Right Source for discernment. We also need to trust the Creator—not the created—not man. The world is full of those who not only reject the Savior, but also full of them who insist on leading souls away from God's ways and go to Satan's counterfeit promises. Believers and nonbelievers alike will all bow the knee before the Judge. Let us now look at the believers' future judgment.

The Judgment Seat of Christ

Believers will be resurrected from the dead just as our Lord Jesus was raised from the dead. But before believers get a new body, their spirits and souls will ascend upward to heaven when the Lord Jesus returns to the clouds to take them up and gather them together in the air. This "taking up" event is customarily known by a word that is not in the Bible. It is traditionally called the *Rapture.*

The Rapture is the next event that will take place in all the prophecies of the Scriptures. We are presently in an era called the "Church Age." This *Age* began on the day called *Pentecost* which came to pass fifty days after the Lord Jesus was resurrected.

The Church Age will end Upon Christ's return to the air to rapture His Church up to heaven. Then the Antichrist will be revealed, and a seven-year Tribulation Period will begin on earth. His return to the air for the Rapture is *not* His Second Coming—also known as His Second Advent (to set foot on the earth). His First Advent took place when the Father sent Him to be born of the virgin Mary, and He was on this earth for thirty-three years as fully God and fully Man. His Second Coming will occur at the end of the seven-year Tribulation Period when He comes to defeat the Antichrist. After that He will begin His Millennial reign. Next, Paul the apostle makes us aware of the imminent Rapture event and will later explain how it saves believers from the wrath of the seven-year Tribulation:

> [13]But I would not have you to be ignorant, brethren concerning them which are asleep [have fallen asleep, in belief, are *dead in Christ*], that ye sorrow not, even as others which have no hope. [14]For if we believe that Jesus died and rose again, even so them also which sleep [have died believing] in Jesus will God bring with him. [15]For this we say unto you by the word of the Lord, that we which are alive *and* remain unto the coming of the Lord shall not prevent [precede] them which are asleep [dead]. [16]For the Lord himself shall descend from heaven with a shout, with the voice of the archangel, and with the trump [trumpet] of God: and the dead in Christ shall rise first: [17]Then we which are alive *and* remain shall be caught up together with them in the clouds, to meet the Lord in the air: and so shall we ever be with the Lord. [18]Wherefore [therefore] comfort one another with these words. 1 Thessalonians 4:13-18

The next chapter, First Thessalonians five, speaks of the *day of the Lord.* The "days of the Lord" are judgment times. The Rapture of the Church in the air, and then the seven-year Tribulation Period on earth are still to come as chapter five begins. Until the sixteenth century there were no chapter and verse separations in the Bible.[32] So the text is a continuation from chapter four. The Rapture *and then* the Tribulation are the next events prophesied. When the seven-year Tribulation ends with the Second Coming of Christ to earth, the event will be followed by His Millennial reign. Scripture warns that when Christ returns at His Second Coming to defeat the Antichrist, He, Jesus, will come like a thief in the night (Matthew

24:43). The Rapture comes in the same manner—it will be a surprise. The ones who did not believe earlier (by the time of the Rapture) will have opportunity, albeit not without tremendous suffering, during the Tribulation period to hear the Gospel message, and some will be saved. But many, despite all the frightful warnings during the Tribulation, will go on believing the Antichrist's deceptions and rejecting the Savior's free offer. First Thessalonians chapter five, after the Rapture explanation in chapter four, reminds the believers of Thessalonica that the Rapture has not yet occurred:

> BUT of the times and the seasons, brethren, ye have no need that I write unto you. [2]For [you] yourselves know perfectly that the day of the Lord so cometh as a thief in the night [This warning could rightfully apply to both the Rapture and the Second Coming]. [3]For when they [unbelievers] say, Peace and safety; then sudden destruction cometh upon them, as travail [labor pains] upon a woman [pregnant woman] with child; and they shall not escape [the wrath]. 1 Thessalonians 5:1-3

Those who will not believe until sometime during the Tribulation Period, are being told that Christ's Second Coming will also be sudden, and it will be a startling event, especially to many who do not seek out the truth of end times prophecy.

The Lord Jesus warns:

> Behold, I come as a thief. Blessed *is* he that watcheth... Revelation 16:15a

> Therefore be ye also ready: for in such an hour as ye think not the Son of man cometh. Matthew 24:44

> [35]Watch ye therefore: for ye know not when the master of the house cometh, at even [evening], or at midnight, or at the cockcrowing, or in the morning: [36]Lest coming

suddenly he find you sleeping. [37]And what I say unto you I say unto all, watch. Mark 13:35-37

But of that day and hour knoweth no *man*, no, not the angels of heaven, but my Father only. Matthew 24:36

Although First Thessalonians chapter five applies to the Rapture, similar wording could also be appropriate for the timing of Christ's Second Coming. No one knows when it will happen, but we must all be ready if we desire to escape the horrific Tribulation Period. People suffering the deceptions and horrors of the Tribulation Period who become familiar with the prophecies may be able to then know the approximate year of the Second Coming, since both Daniel 7:25; 9:27; 12:7, 11 and Revelation 11:2, 3; 12:14; 13:5 give three and one-half more years from after the idol image [the *abomination of desolation*] is set up in the temple. Due to the uncertainty of the day and hour of either the Rapture or the Second Coming, we should be prepared to meet our Maker.

Prepare to meet thy God. Amos 4:12b

"The knowledge of this will be more useful than to know the exact time, because this should awaken us to stand upon our watch, that we may be ready whenever he cometh."[33]

Take ye heed, watch and pray: for ye know not when the time is. Mark 13:33

Then chapter five goes on to say that they who come to believe should be confident:

[4]But ye, brethren [all believers], are not in darkness, that that day should overtake you as a thief. [5]Ye are all the

children of light, and the children of the day: we are not of the night, nor of darkness. [6]Therefore let us not sleep, as do others; but let us watch and be sober [self-controlled]. [7]For they that sleep sleep in the night; and they that be drunken are drunken in the night, [8]But let us, who are of the day, be sober, putting on the breastplate of faith and love; and for a helmet, the hope of salvation. [9]For God hath not appointed us to wrath, but to obtain salvation by our Lord Jesus Christ, [10]who died for us, that, whether we wake or sleep, we should live together with him. [11]Wherefore comfort [encourage] yourselves [each other] together, and edify [build up] one another, even as also ye do [are doing].

1 Thessalonians 5:4-11

Verse nine does *not* say that those who finally come to believe during the Tribulation period will not suffer wrath. They will indeed be here on earth to experience it. However, they will be saved for heaven and from the final judgment of the Lake of Fire.

What verse nine does tell believers of the Church Age is that they will be raptured and will not suffer the deceptions and wrath of the seven-year Tribulation Period. Romans 5:9 agrees with 1 Thessalonians 5:9:

[8]But God commendeth his [demonstrates His own] love toward us, in that, while we were yet sinners, Christ died for us. [9]Much more then, being now [having been] justified [justified to be seen as righteous in God's view] by his blood, we shall be saved from wrath through him [Jesus Christ]. Romans 5:8-9

And to wait for his Son from heaven, whom he raised from the dead, *even* Jesus, which delivered us from the wrath to come. 1 Thessalonians 1:10

First Corinthians chapter fifteen also foretells the Rapture:

[51]Behold, I show you a mystery; We shall not all sleep [be in our graves], but we shall all be changed, [52]In a moment, in the twinkling of an eye, at the last trump [last *trumpet* signifying the end of the Church Age]: for the trumpet shall sound, and the dead shall be raised incorruptible, and we shall be changed.
1 Corinthians 15:51-52

The Savior tells us He is coming to take us up to heaven:

LET not your heart be troubled: ye believe in God, believe also in me. [2]In my Father's house [heaven] are many mansions [dwellings]: if *it were* not *so*, I would have told you. I go to prepare a place for you. [3]And if I go and prepare a place for you, I will come again, and receive you unto myself; that where I am *there* ye may be also. John 14:1-3

All believers will be blessed with a new, glorious body:

[20]For our conversation [citizenship] is in heaven; from whence also we look for the Savior, the Lord Jesus Christ: [21]Who shall change our vile body, that it may be fashioned like unto his glorious body, according to the working whereby he is able even to subdue all things unto himself. Philippians 3:20-21

No man knows when the Rapture, the seven-year Tribulation, or the Second Coming will take place. No one other than the Father God knows. Our God and Savior Jesus said this:

> But of that day and *that* hour knoweth no man, no, not the angels which are in heaven, neither the Son, but the Father. Mark 13:32

Although some biblical scholars maintain that the Rapture will not take place until mid-tribulation, and some even insist that it will occur at post-tribulation, the chronological order given in Revelation chapters four through seven reveal that the believers of the Church Age are taken up prior to the Tribulation Period and others come to believe during the Tribulation. Immediately after the churches are spoken to in chapters two and three, chapter four has the prophecy of the universal church being raptured, and chapter five tells of how the raptured ones will be worshiping and praising:

> AFTER this [after the churches are spoken to] I looked, and, behold, a door *was* opened in heaven: and the first voice which I heard *was* as it were of a trumpet talking with me; which said, Come up hither, and I will show thee things which must be hereafter [the *things which must be hereafter* are the praising in chapter five, then the revealing of the Antichrist in chapter six, and then the ones who will be saved during the Tribulation in chapter seven.]. Revelation 4:1

> And they [the elders] had on their heads crowns of gold. [the church elders obviously had their new bodies which are promised in Philippians 3:21 if they had *heads* on which to wear their *crowns*.]. Revelation 4:4b

> [9a]And they sung a new song, saying, Thou art worthy ... [9c]for thou wast slain, and hast redeemed us to God by

thy blood out of every kindred, and tongue, and people, and nation; Revelation 5:9a, c

And I beheld, and I heard the voice of many angels round about the throne and the beasts [margin and NKJV gives *living creatures*; and 2 Corinthians 5:17a tells us "*Therefore if any man be in Christ, he is a new creature*" so these *beasts* are the members of the raptured Church] and the elders: and the number of them was ten thousand times ten thousand, and thousands of thousands; Revelation 5:11

The sixth chapter then reveals the Antichrist's seven-year career as he arrives on four different colored horses which represent the four segments of his regime: a white horse for *peace*, a red horse for power to conduct conflict and violence, a black horse for enormous inflation and famine, and a pale horse for the Antichrist and his followers' deaths.

Chapter seven, then, brings to our attention the saving of the 144,000 of the tribes of Israel. These thousands will then spread the Gospel message helping to lead numberless multitudes to the Lord *during the Tribulation*. It is noteworthy that the next words of the passage following that of the 144,000 begin with these words: *After this*:

[9]After this I beheld , and, lo, a great multitude, which no man could number, of all nations, and kindreds [tribes], and people, and tongues [languages], stood before the throne, and before the Lamb, clothed with white robes, and palms in their hands ...

[13]And one of the elders answered, saying unto me, What are these which are arrayed in white robes? And whence came they? [14]And I said unto him, Sir, thou knowest. And he said to me, These are they which came out

of great tribulation, and have washed their robes, and made them white in the blood of the Lamb.
Revelation 7:9, 13-14

The orderly chronological order of events given in chapters, two through seven, convincingly point to the fact that the Rapture occurs prior to the coming of the Antichrist and thus, prior to the beginning of his Tribulation Period career. Daniel prophesied that the Antichrist would first be revealed by offering a peace treaty; this is in agreement with Revelation 6:2 where the Antichrist first appears on the *white* horse:

> And he [the Antichrist] shall confirm the covenant [a treaty] with many for one week [A *week* in Hebrew translates to *seven years* in this usage]. Daniel 9:27a

Paul also prophesied that the Antichrist would be restrained from being revealed until after the Church—indwelled by the Holy Spirit—is raptured:

> [6]And now ye know what withholdeth [is restraining] that he [the Antichrist] might be revealed in his time [Tribulation period]. [7]For the mystery [hidden truth] of iniquity [lawlessness] doth already work: only he [the Holy Spirit indwelled Church] who now letteth [restrains] *will let* [will do], until he [the Church] be taken [raptured] out of the way. [8a]And then shall that Wicked be revealed... 2 Thessalonians 2:6-8a

When the human body dies, the spirit and soul are separated from the body which eventually rots. The spirit and soul continue on forever—either in eternal suffering—or everlasting life...depending upon one's rejection or acceptance of the Savior.

Believers will be judged by the Lord Jesus at the Judgment Seat of Christ for rewards or lack there of:

> [6]Therefore *we are* always confident, knowing that, whilst we are at home in the body, we are absent from the Lord: [7](For we walk by faith, not by sight:) [8]We are confident, *I say*, and willing rather to be absent from the body, and to be present with the Lord. [9]Wherefore we labor [make it our aim], that, whether present or absent, we may be accepted of him [well pleasing to God]. [10]For we must all appear before the judgment seat of Christ; that every one may receive the things *done* in *his* body, according to that he hath done, whether *it be* good or bad. 2 Corinthians 5:6-10

> Rejoice ye in that day, and leap for joy: for, behold, your reward *is* great in heaven. Luke 6:23a

> Now he that planteth [he who explains the Gospel message to others] and he that watereth [continue the growth of the ones who hear the Gospel message] are one: and every man shall receive his own reward according to his own labor. 1 Corinthians 3:8

> If any man's work abide [endures] which he hath built thereupon, he shall receive a reward. 1 Corinthians 3:14

> And whatsoever ye do, do *it* heartily, as to the Lord, and not unto men; knowing that of the Lord ye shall receive the reward of the inheritance: for ye serve the Lord Christ. Colossians 3:23-24

The Lord Jesus Christ is quoted in the last chapter of the Bible:

And, behold, I come quickly; and my reward *is* with me, to give every man according as his work shall be. Revelation 22:12

In the first chapter in the last book of the Bible, we read this: For the time is at hand. Revelation 1:3b

Now that we have reviewed the believers' judgment, let us see what is in store for those who will go on rejecting the Savior.

The Great White Throne Judgment

Believers aren't the only ones who will be raised back from being dead. The unsaved will also be resurrected from their graves to face the Lord Jesus for judgment at the Great White Throne to receive their "reward" — to be doomed:

[11]And I saw a great white throne, and him that sat on it, from whose face the earth and the heaven fled away; and there was found no place for them. [12]And I saw the dead, small and great, stand before God; and another book was opened, which is *the book* of life: and the dead were judged out of those things which were written in the books, according to their works. [13]And the sea gave up the dead which were in it; and death and hell [hādēs] delivered up the dead which were in them: and they were judged every man according to their works. [14]And death and hell [hādēs] were cast into the lake of fire. This is the second death. [15]And whosoever was not found written in the book of life was cast into the lake of fire. Revelation 20:11-15

[12]But these, as natural brute beasts, made to be taken [caught] and destroyed, speak evil of the things that they understand not; and shall utterly perish in their own corruption; [13]And shall receive the reward [wages] of unrighteousness, *as* they that count it pleasure to riot [revel, feast with clamorous merriment] in the daytime. Spots *they are* and blemishes, sporting themselves with their own deceivings while they feast with you; [14]Having eyes full of adultery, and that cannot cease from sin; beguiling [enticing] unstable souls: a heart they have exercised [trained] with covetous practices; cursed children: [15a]Which have forsaken the right way and are gone astray. 2 Peter 2:12-15a

For the wages of sin *is* death; but the gift of God *is* eternal life through Jesus Christ our Lord. Romans 6:23

The most minuscule degree of discernment enlightens one to at least ask the question, "What if this is true?" Since God inspired the Scriptures that are pure, flawless, and with no contradictions, these judgments are the truth. Anyone or anything that contradicts God's Word must be looked upon with discernment:

Now I beseech you, brethren, mark [note] them which cause divisions and offenses contrary to the doctrine which ye have learned; and avoid them. Romans 16:17

Chapter 6

Discernment Demands Awareness

Beware of false prophets [false teachers], which come to you in sheep's clothing, but inwardly they are ravening [ravenous] wolves. Matthew 7:15

Three of the twelve apostles whom were chosen by the Lord Jesus, Paul, Peter, and John, reinforce the warnings that Christ has given. Paul is quoted speaking to the local church elders:

[28]Take heed therefore unto yourselves, and to all the flock [the believing people, the local church], over the which the Holy Ghost hath made you overseers, to feed [shepherd] the church of God, which he hath purchased with his own blood. [29]For I know this, that after my departing shall grievous [savage] wolves enter in among you, not sparing the flock. Acts 20:28-29

Peter is quoted as he begins to write to all who believe and have *precious* faith—valuable faith—which protects us from false teachers:

SIMON Peter, a servant and on apostle of Jesus Christ, to them that have obtained like [the same] precious faith with us through the righteousness of [our Father] God and our [God and] Savior Jesus Christ. 2 Peter 1:1

BUT there were false prophets also among the people, even as there shall be false teachers among you, who privily [secretly] shall bring in damnable [destructive] heresies [contradictions to God's teachings], even denying the Lord that bought them, and bring upon themselves swift destruction. 2 Peter 2:1

John also writes to all believers urging them to "test the spirits" to discern whether or not the teachers are teaching the truth or falsehoods.

BELOVED, believe not every spirit, but try [test] the spirits whether they are of God: because many false prophets are gone out into the world. 1 John 4:1

These warnings were true nearly 2,000 years ago when the apostles wrote about it, and false teaching is still prevalent today.

The word *doctrine* means, "in the general sense, *whatever is taught.*"[34]

Whatever is taught can include false teaching. There are several disagreements about the curriculum for children from kindergarten level to elementary, middle school, high school, and even adults in colleges and universities. *Doctrine* has been *indoctrinating* thousands upon thousands of students into forsaking the Bible's sound doctrine and accepting *man's* many contrasting principles.

The diversifying doctrines lead not only to confusion and division, but even to violent methods of protesting. This further develops into dividing nations, societies, communities, churches, and even families. Simply for reason of another's belief, some people are roused to hate—especially those who are at odds with Christ to the point of an entire lifelong rejection of Him.

Jesus said:

> Blessed are ye, when men shall hate you, and when they shall separate you *from their company*, and shall reproach [revile, insult] *you*, and cast out your name as evil, for the Son of Man's [Christ's] sake. Luke 6:22

> [34]Think not that I am come to send peace on earth: I came not to send peace, but a sword. [35]For I am come to SET A MAN AT VARIANCE AGAINST HIS FATHER, AND THE DAUGHTER AGAINST HER MOTHER, AND THE DAUGHTER-IN-LAW AGAINST HER MOTHER-IN-LAW. [36]And A MAN'S FOES *SHALL BE* THEY OF HIS OWN HOUSEHOLD. Matthew 10:34-36 (Jesus quoted Micah 7:6)

> [51]Suppose ye that I am come to give peace on earth? I tell you, Nay; but rather division: [52]For from henceforth there shall be five in one house divided, three against two, and two against three. [53]The father shall be divided against the son, and the son against the father; the mother against the daughter, and the daughter against the mother; the mother-in-law against her daughter-in-law, and the daughter-in-law against her mother-in-law. Luke 12:51-53

Children instilled with false teachings can result in major obstacles to their ability to discern the truth. Once indoctrinated, people have a natural resistance to change.

Creation or Evolution?

Children grow to become adults either believing each new human has been reincarnated, has evolved from *nothing* at all to *something* better as time goes on; or else they believe life has been transferred from one generation to the next by procreation. What does God say about this?

> Male and female created he them; and blessed them, and called their name Adam [Mankind], in the day when they were created. Genesis 5:2

> [6]The words of the LORD *are* pure words: *as* silver tried in a furnace of earth, purified seven times. [7]Thou shalt keep them, O LORD, thou shalt preserve them from this generation for ever. Psalm 12:6-7

> [5]Every word of God *is* pure [tried, found pure]: he *is* a shield unto them that put their trust in him. [6]Add thou not unto his words, lest he reprove [convict] thee, and thou be found a liar. Proverbs 30:5-6

There are 404 verses in the Book of Revelation, 265 of which refer to 550 Old Testament passages or verses.

Our Creator is serious about the fact when He says He is our Creator:

> [18]For I testify unto every man that heareth the words of the prophecy of this book, If any man shall add unto these things, God shall add unto him the plagues that are written in this book: [19]And if any man shall take away from the words of the book of this prophecy, God

shall take away his part out of the book of life, and out of the holy city [heaven], and *from* the things which are written in this book. Revelation 22:18-19

William MacDonald writes:

"Since the subjects in this book are woven through-out the Bible, the verse (Revelation 22:18-19), in effect, condemns any tampering with God's word. A suitable judgment is pronounced on anyone who takes away from the words of this prophecy. This does not apply to minor differences of interpretation, but to an outright attack on the inspiration and completeness of the Bible. The penalty is eternal doom. God shall take away his part from the tree of life (NKJV margin). It means that he will never share in the blessings of those who have eternal life."[35]

In Genesis 1:28 where God told man and woman to multiply the population on this earth, even secular history gives a true picture that generations have been caused by the reproductive increases. His Word speaks of *generation* and *generations* over 200 times. Here are but a few examples:

And *that* these days *should be* remembered and kept throughout every generation, every family, every province, and every city; Esther 9:28a

[3]Great *is* the LORD, and greatly to be praised; and his greatness *is* unsearchable [beyond our understanding]. [4]One generation shall praise thy works to another, and shall declare thy mighty acts. Psalm 145:3-4

One generation passeth away, and *another* generation cometh: Ecclesiastes 1:4a

[7]Hearken [Listen] unto me, ye that know righteousness, the people in whose heart *is* my law; fear ye not the reproach of men, neither be ye afraid of their revilings [insults]. [8]For the moth shall eat them like wool: but my righteousness shall be for ever, and my salvation from generation to generation. Isaiah 51:7-8

Thou, O LORD, remainest for ever, thy throne from generation to generation. Lamentations 5:19

How great *are* his signs! And how mighty *are* his wonders! His kingdom *is* an everlasting kingdom, and his dominion *is* from generation to generation. Daniel 4:3

Tell ye your children of it, and *let* your children *tell* their children, and their children another generation. Joel 1:3

So all the generations from Abraham to David *are* fourteen generations; and from David unto the carrying away into Babylon *are* fourteen generations; and from the carrying away into Babylon unto Christ *are* fourteen generations. Matthew 1:17

Most families that have had children have helped to exponentially multiply the earth's population for over 4,000 years —that is, since about two hundred years after the flood in Noah's time. At conception, life has been transferred again and again, and each one of us is living proof of it. Many offspring resemble their parents in looks and in sounds of their voices...not to mention having the parents' DNA.

From approximately 3,400 years ago, God inspired words covering more than a 1,500-year time span to be written in the Old Testament. Even into the New Testament, He supernaturally caused all forty writers of the entire Bible, totally nearly 1,600 years, to be in miraculous agreement. And He had them write that He, the eternal God, is, indeed, Creator of everything.

When Charles Darwin wrote his book, *Origin of the Species*, only 160 years ago (note, only 1/10th of the time span from 1,600 to 160 years), he urged the intellectual philosophers and professors to teach that it is factual that there is no creator; and that everything in the universe simply evolved from *nothing*.

A person who possesses discernment should easily see the problem with the latter. But let's look even closer:

> IN the beginning God created the heaven and the earth. [2]And the earth was without form, and void; and darkness *was* upon the face of the deep. And the Spirit of God moved upon the face of the waters. [3]And God said, Let there be light. Genesis 1:1-3

As we compare Scripture to Scripture, we see that all three Persons of God were present when creation occurred. The Father was the One who said, "Let there be light," the Son was the Creator who obeyed the command and made the light, (Genesis 1:6-8; Psalm 19:1; Isaiah 40:22; John 1:1-5; Colossians 1:16-17; Hebrews 1:1-3, 10), and we read here in Genesis 1:2, "the Spirit of God moved upon the face of the waters."

In chapter one of this book, *Developing Discernment*, John 1:1-2; Colossians 1:14-19; and Hebrews 1:1-10 were given, and those verses inform us of the power of God to create everything. The Father gives credit to the Son for being the Creator.

If those who opt to reject the righteous Creator and who insist upon not listening to God's truths, God's inspired Word gives us the following dire news:

> [18]For the wrath of God is revealed from heaven against all ungodliness and unrighteousness of men, who hold

[suppress] the truth in unrighteousness; [19]Because that which may be known of God is manifest [evident] in them [among them]; for God hath showed *it* unto them. [20]For the invisible things of him from the creation of the world are clearly seen, being understood by the things that are made, *even* his eternal power and God-head [divine nature]; so that they [those who reject Him] are without excuse: [21]Because that, when they knew God, they glorified *him* not as God, neither were thankful; but became vain [futile] in their imaginations [thoughts], and their foolish heart was darkened. [22]Professing themselves to be wise, they became fools. Romans 1:18-22

"In order to express His nature (holiness, truth, and justice), God must punish sin. Since sin personally offends God, no one should be surprised that sin makes God angry. To deny His anger is to reject the necessity of Christ's reconciling work on the cross. God's wrath is revealed both in nature and in the Scriptures. **Illustration:** [God's] rage that today is vented against sin will someday be completely unleashed in hell against those who refuse to accept [the Father's] satisfaction (a satisfaction which is called *propitiation*) that Christ made on the cross. **Application:** Since this propitiation by Christ suffices for the whole world, there is no reason anyone should spend eternity in hell unless he voluntarily rejects God's truth."[36]

As God's anger—or wrath—is satisfied to justify a man as having God's righteousness based solely upon the man's belief that the Savior's shed blood has forgiven him. God's satisfaction in this relationship is called *propitiation*. Along with belief in Christ's resurrection, the believer is then joined together in unity with God.

Since this chapter is purposed to compare creation to evolution, Romans 1:20 above should be repeated and accompanied with explanation:

> For the invisible things of him from the creation of the world are clearly seen, being understood by the things that are made, *even* his eternal power and Godhead [divine nature]; so that they [those who reject Him] are without excuse. Romans 1:20

> "The cosmological argument to the existence of God leads to the physics of cause and effect. God's existence is logical because everything that exists must have an adequate cause, so an all-powerful and intelligent Creator is an adequate cause to explain the universe."[37]

The Scriptures, Genesis 1:1, Romans 1:19-20, John 1:1-3, Hebrews 1:1-14, plus others, confirm that God is indeed our Creator. And He truly loves us and gives us hope.

A Christian hymn often sung to children is "Jesus loves me! This I know, for the Bible tells me so." Singing to the same tune, Christian comedian, Tim Hawkins, changes the wording: "Nobody loves me! This I know. Charles Darwin told me so."

And quoting Pat Boone's statement in the movie, *God's Not Dead 2*: "The problem with atheism is that it doesn't take away the pain; it only takes away the hope."

Not only has God created us in our beginning and will therefore always love us, but He also newly creates us after He separates us from the bondage of sin upon our sincerely acknowledging Him:

> [17]Therefore if any man *be* in Christ, *he is* a new creature [creation]: old things are passed away; behold, all things

are become new. [18a]And all things *are* of God, who reconciled us to himself by Jesus Christ.
2 Corinthians 5:17-18a

When man believes in and is united with the risen and
glorified Savior, he is a new creation. We cannot help our God
to win souls away from Satan and to win souls for the Father
until we are created in Jesus Christ, who tells us:

> I am the vine, ye *are* the branches: He that abideth in
> me, and I in him, the same bringeth forth much fruit:
> for without me ye can do nothing. John 15:5

When a grapevine is well-rooted, then the branches can
produce fruit—that is, healthy branches can help other
new branches to come about—branches which will produce
fruit—grapes. Looking at it from a spiritual perspective, mature
believers can be fruitful to help lead others to a life-changing
relationship with Jesus Christ and help develop the new believers in their walk with the Lord.

> [6]As ye have therefore received Christ Jesus the Lord, *so*
> walk *ye* in him: [7]Rooted and built up in him, and stab-
> lished in the faith, as ye have been taught, abounding
> therein with thanksgiving. Colossians 2:6-7
>
> THERE *is* therefore now no condemnation to them
> which are in Christ Jesus, who walk not after the flesh,
> but after the Spirit. Romans 8:1

When believers are *in Christ Jesus*, indwelt by the Holy
Spirit of God, they are still sinners. Quoting Randy Amos,
"they are not sinless, but they do sin less." We can only be
a worthy representative of God when we have been divinely

transformed into being a new creation. Since He is presently at the right hand of the Father in heaven, He relies upon us to be His instruments here on earth to lead others, to reconcile others to again be at one with God—atoned for—reconciled— redeemed:

> And all things *are* of God, who hath reconciled us to himself by Jesus Christ, and hath given to us the ministry of reconciliation; 2 Corinthians 5:18

> [20]Now then we are ambassadors for Christ, as though God did beseech *you* by us: we pray [implore] *you* in Christ's stead [behalf], be ye reconciled to God. [21]For he hath made him *to be* sin for us, who knew no sin; that we might be made the righteousness of God in him. 2 Corinthians 5:20-21

Treat Everyone Like They Won't Be Here Tomorrow

How often and how sad it is to hear of people unexpectedly and instantly losing their lives to tragic accidents, shootings, or any vital failures within the body.

This unwelcome fact takes us to the *Golden Rule*: "Do unto others as you would have others do unto you."

The Lord Jesus our Savior said it like this:

> And as ye would that men should do to you, do ye also to them likewise. Luke 6:31

That is the most repeated *rule* from the Old Testament (Deuteronomy 6:5) to the New Testament. It follows the *Great Commandment* in which the Lord Jesus said:

> THOU SHALT LOVE THE LORD THY GOD WITH ALL THY HEART, AND WITH ALL THY SOUL, AND WITH

ALL THY MIND, AND WITH ALL THY STRENGTH: Mark 12:30

The *Golden Rule* was first given by our Lord and God like this: Thou shalt not avenge [take vengeance], nor bear any grudge against the children of thy people, but thou shalt love thy neighbor as thyself: I *am* the LORD. Leviticus 19:18

The other eight times we are told to love our neighbor as ourselves: Matthew 7:12a; Luke 6:31; Matthew 19:19b; Matthew 22:39b; Mark 12:31b; Luke 10:27b, c; Romans 13:9b; Galatians 5:14b; James 2:8b.

The question arises, "Who is my neighbor?"

Our neighbor is anyone in need of anything we have and that he does not have. If they do not possess the life changing relationship with the Lord Jesus which the believer has, then the saved man should love his neighbor by sharing the message of eternal life.

Love the Sinner / Hate the Sin

Our Lord God Himself hates sin. A perfect example of this is given when God refers to His second of the Ten Commandments telling us to *have no other gods before Him and to not be idolaters idolizing created images.* God is a jealous God who hates sin:

Neither shalt thou set thee up *any* image [idol]; which the LORD thy God hateth. Deuteronomy 16:22

God hates any and all sin against any of His Commandments. In His ninth Commandment He teaches us it is a sin to
even tell a lie:

> Neither shalt thou bear false witness against thy neigh-
> bor. Deuteronomy 5:20

Besides the false teaching of evolution, another indoctrination of the world's children today is the falsehood of making
them think they were born in such a way that offends God.
Man teaches that they were created (or maybe even evolved)
to be something other than the ever so true evidence of
their biological birth. The community of the modern culture
which supports this teaching demands that Christians be *tolerant*. Therefore, desiring to be seen as good representatives
of Christ, to be loving and understanding, many Christians are
subtly coerced into condoning—not believing, but excusing
the falsehood.

A true believer does not want to do harm to anyone—
period. A true Christian is taught to love his neighbor.

Again the neighbor is anyone who is in need of something
which the Christian has to offer.

What the person needs, who has been falsely taught...is love
—and eternal life. That's what God and his believing Church
desires to put forward. Therefore, the Church asks the LGBTQ+
community to be *tolerant* to hear them out. What does the
Creator have to say about it? Would one be willing to listen?

The loving Savior came to bear the truth.

Upfront this is going to sound very grim and depressing,
but one must read to near the end of this chapter in order to
realize the *eternal hope* that is freely offered to everyone, no
matter what he has done.

The LORD our God spoke this:

You shall not lie with a male as with a woman. It *is* an abomination [The word *abomination* expresses that which is repulsive, detestable, or offensive.].
Leviticus 18:22 NKJV

Neither shalt thou lie with any beast to defile thyself therewith: neither shall any woman stand before a beast to lie down thereto: it is confusion [perversion]."
Leviticus 18:23

If a man lies with a male as he lies with a woman, both of them have committed an abomination. They shall surely be put to death. Their blood shall be upon them.
Leviticus 20:13 NKJV

They must be *put to death*; their blood will be on their own heads. Here it is so crucial, yes, absolutely essential, to remember and understand that Christ Jesus took the sin upon Himself and died in the place of every sinner. But only the sinner who is willing to admit his guilt and *sincerely* seek the Lord's forgiveness will be saved.

For the wages of sin *is* death, but the gift of God *is* eternal life through [*in* Christ Jesus] Jesus Christ our Lord.
Romans 6:23

The *death* that's being cited is referred to again in the last Book of the Bible. This *death* spoken of here is actually the *second death*:

the...sexually immoral...shall have their part in the lake which burns with fire and brimstone, which is the second death. Revelation 21:8b. NIV

This Scripture is provided with deepest heartfelt, sensitive love for sinners to make them aware of the consequences for trading temporary pleasure for eternal life.

Our Lord Jesus Christ, if we do not reject Him, and if we accept Him as our Savior with a sincere heart of repentance, will forgive us and provide *eternal life* with Him in God's kingdom—heaven.

> [9]Know ye not that the unrighteous shall not inherit the kingdom [heaven] of God? Be not deceived: neither fornicators [sexually immoral], nor idolaters [worshipers of any idol instead of God], nor adulterers, nor effeminate [homosexuals], nor abusers [sodomites] of themselves with mankind, [10]Nor thieves, nor covetous, nor drunkards, nor revilers, nor extortioners, shall inherit the kingdom of God. [11]And such were some of you [believers]: but ye are washed, but ye are sanctified [now *set apart* from the world], but ye are justified [declared righteous] in the name of the Lord Jesus, and by the Spirit of our God. 1 Corinthians 6:9-11

> [8]But we know that the law [the Ten Commandments] *is* good, if a man use it lawfully; [9]Knowing this, that the law is not made for a righteous man, but for the lawless and disobedient, for the ungodly and for sinners, for unholy and profane, for murderers of fathers and murderers of mothers, for manslayers, [10]For whoremongers [fornicators], for them that defile themselves [sodomites] with mankind, for menstealers [kidnappers], for liars, for perjured persons [perjurers], and if there be any other thing that is contrary to sound doctrine; [11]According to the glorious gospel of the blessed God, which was committed to my trust.
> 1 Timothy 1:8-11

With modern day indoctrination there are thousands upon thousands of minds being corrupted—not only by teachers and professors, but also by high level politicians:

> During a Senate Hearing for filling a U.S. Supreme Court vacancy, U.S. Senator Mazie Hirono from Hawaii, on October 13, 2020, called out Judge Amy Coney Barrett for using the expression *sexual preference.* "Sexual preference is an offensive and outdated term, it is used by anti-LGBTQ activists to suggest that sexual orientation is a choice—it is not," the Hawaii Democrat said.[38]

> "At 9:44 PM, Oct 13, 2020 the following Twitter message was posted: 'As recently as last month, Webster's Dictionary included a definition of "preference" as "orientation" or sexual preference.' TODAY they changed it and added the word "offensive." Insane—I just checked through Wayback Machine and it's real."[39]

> Within twenty-four hours—[do not miss this]—*after* what seemed more like an *interrogation* by Senator Hirono, *Merriam Webster* posted the addition of the expression to include "offensive". The *Merriam Webster*'s editor-at-large explained in a statement to Fox News: "In this case, we released the update for sexual preference when we noticed that the entries for preference and sexual preference were being consulted in connection with the SCOTUS [Supreme Court of the U.S.] hearings. A revision made in response to an entry's increased attention differs only in celerity" [velocity]—"as always, all revisions reflect evidence of use."[40]

The scolding should be given to Senator Hirono for this uncalled for, unfair, despicable conduct. She tried to put Judge Amy Barrett into a political *preference* of the senator's own foul play, even coercing Judge Barrett into making an apology (an apology that most likely went against Judge Barrett's own faith).

It is interesting to note that neither the *1828 Noah Webster Dictionary of the English Language* nor the 1971 *New Webster Dictionary of the English Language* include this *new* revelation. Indoctrinated students might be thinking that their professors have made new discoveries having to do with gender identification, homosexuals, and fornicators. But God's Word reminds us:

> [9]The thing that hath been, it *is that* which shall be; and that which is done *is* that which shall be done: and *there is* no new *thing* under the sun. [10]Is there *any* thing whereof it may be said, See, this *is* new? it hath been already of old time [in ancient times] which was before us. Ecclesiastes 1:9-10

Henry Ironside said, "If it is new it is not true; if it is true it is not new."

Not only is it offensive to the LGBT community in man's view, but for anyone of God's creation to prefer this unnatural orientation rather than His creative intent, it results in grieving the Holy Spirit of God. Furthermore, it grieves the Spirit within each and every true believer due to knowing the eternal suffering that is in store for those who offend God with this disrespect. Whichever way you look at it, others and Someone will be offended. There will be division when man's way interferes with God's way.

When God created the male and female, He expected them to continue in the form He created. He separates Himself from the transgender agenda:

> [14]I know that, whatsoever God doeth, it shall be for ever: nothing can be put [added] to it, nor any thing taken

from it: and God doeth *it*, that *men* should fear before him. [15]That which hath been is now; and that which is to be hath already been: and God requireth that which is past [explanation to Him of your past].
Ecclesiastes 3:14-15

For I *am* the LORD, I change not... Malachi 3:6a

But the WORD OF THE LORD ENDURETH FOR EVER...
1 Peter 1:25a

And I saw a great white throne, and him [Jesus] that sat on it... Revelation 20:11a

That at the name of Jesus every knee should bow...
Philippians 2:10a

And whosoever was not found written in the book of life was cast into the lake of fire [the Lake of Fire is the *second death* which lasts forever (Revelation 21:8)].
Revelation 20:15

Committing sin as a homosexual has been going on just as long as the sin of the adulterer—ever since before even Noah and Abraham's times. The pure Word of God takes us back to Sodom and Gomorrah:

[4]But before they [two angel men who visited Lot's house in the city of Sodom] lay down, the men of the city, *even* the men of Sodom, compassed [surrounded] the house round, both old and young, all the people from every quarter: [5]And they called unto Lot, and said unto him, Where *are* the men which came in to thee this night? Bring them out unto us, that we may know them [know them carnally, have sex with them]. [6]And Lot

went out at the door unto them, and shut the door after him, ⁷And said, I pray you, brethren, do not so wickedly. ⁸Behold now, I have two daughters which have not known man [virgins]; let me, I pray you, bring them out unto you, and do ye to them as *is* good in your eyes [as you wish]: only unto these men do nothing; for therefore came they under the shadow of my roof. ⁹And they [the men of Sodom] said, Stand back. And they said *again*, This one *fellow* came in to sojourn [stay a little while], and he will needs be [keeps acting as] a judge: now will we deal worse with thee, than with them. And they pressed sore [mightily] upon the man, *even* Lot, and came near to break the door. ¹⁰But the men [the two angel men] put forth their hand, and pulled Lot into the house to them, and shut to the door. Genesis 19:4-10

And it came to pass, when they had brought them forth abroad [outside], that he [*they*, the angel men] said, Escape for thy life; look not behind thee, neither stay thou in all the plain; escape to the mountain, lest thou be consumed [destroyed]. Genesis 19:17

²⁴Then the LORD rained upon Sodom and upon Gomorrah brimstone and fire from the LORD out of heaven; ²⁵And he overthrew [devastated] those cities, and all the plain, and all the inhabitants of the cities, and that which grew upon the ground. ²⁶But his [Lot's] wife looked back from behind him, and she became a pillar of salt. Genesis 19:24-26

And he [Abraham—Lot's uncle] looked toward Sodom and Gomorrah, and toward all the land of the plain, and beheld, and, lo, the smoke of the country went up as the smoke of a furnace. Genesis 19:28

That's the Old Testament account of what happened to Sodom and Gomorrah because of the immoral sexual sin in those cities.

> [6]Now these things were [became] our examples, to the intent we should not lust after evil things, as they also lusted. ...
>
> [11]Now all these things happened unto them for examples: and they are written for our admonition [instruction], upon whom the ends of the world are come.
> 1 Corinthians 10:6, 11

The New Testament provides a comparison to the Sodom and Gomorrah event with what will take place in the end:

> [6]And the [fallen] angels which kept not their first estate [proper domain in heaven in Genesis 6:1-4—rather came down to earth], but left their own habitation, he [God] hath reserved in everlasting chains under darkness unto the judgment of the great day. [7]Even as Sodom and Gomorrah, and the cities about them in like manner, giving themselves over to fornication [sexual immorality], and going after strange flesh [men with men], are set forth for an example, suffering the vengeance [punishment] of eternal fire. Jude 6-7

> [4]For if God spared not the [fallen] angels that sinned, but cast *them* down to hell, and delivered *them* into chains of darkness, to be reserved unto judgment; [5]And spared not the old world, but saved Noah the eighth person, a preacher of righteousness, bringing in the flood upon the world of the ungodly; [6]And turning the cities of Sodom and Gomorrah into ashes condemned them with an overthrow [to destruction], making *them* an example unto those that after [afterward] should

live ungodly; [7]And delivered just Lot, vexed [oppressed] with the filthy conversation [conduct] of the wicked: [8](For that righteous man dwelling among them, in seeing and hearing, vexed [tormented] *his* righteous soul from day to day with *their* unlawful deeds;) [9]The Lord knoweth how to deliver the godly out of temptations, and to reserve the unjust unto the day of judgment to be punished: [10]But chiefly them that walk after [according to] the flesh in the lust of uncleanness, and despise government [authority]. Presumptuous *are they*, self-willed, they are not afraid to speak evil of dignities [dignitaries]. 2 Peter 2:4-10

Attempting a Loving Approach

How can one articulate love with a person who has been led by false teachings (has been indoctrinated) and thinks in her own heart that she is doing what is compassionate and humane? It truly does not matter whether we are man or woman, or black or white, citizen or foreigner, or tall or short. We have all offended God:

> For all have sinned, and come short of the glory of God;
> Romans 3:23

No matter what any person has done, God loves each and every one of us so very much [He created us. He makes each one of His believes feel like she is the only one that matters], and He just wants us to really know Him. When one knows Him, he will love Him.

Here's how the Spirit of God led Paul the apostle to say it:

> This is a faithful saying, and worthy of all acceptation, that Christ Jesus came into the world to save sinners; of whom I am chief. 1 Timothy 1:15

> For I could wish that myself were accursed from Christ for my brethren, my kinsmen according to the flesh: Romans 9:3

That is truly remarkable! Paul was willing to give up his own salvation for the other people to be saved in his stead. He loved his unbelieving Israelite brothers and sisters more than he loved himself. He loved them so much that he was willing to suffer the eternal punishment for their sins.

Paul also admitted that he was the chief sinner of them all—probably because he, Paul—who was called *Saul* prior to going by his Greek name, *Paul*—knew he himself was an accomplice with those who were murdering Christians shortly before he was saved. And, get this: he was chosen by the Lord Jesus to be one of His apostles:

> AND Saul [Paul] was consenting unto his [Steven's] death. At that time there was [arose] a great persecution against the church which was at Jerusalem. Acts 8:1a

> [15]But the Lord said unto him, Go thy way: for he [Paul] is a chosen vessel unto me, to bear my name before the Gentiles, and kings, and the children of Israel: [16]For I will show him how great things he must suffer for my name's sake. Acts 9:15-16

After the Lord Jesus got his attention on the road to Damascus, Paul began to see the truth and quickly grew to be more and more Christlike. Paul writes:

> [6]For when we were yet without strength, in due time [at the right time] Christ died for the ungodly. [7]For scarcely for a righteous man will one die: yet per adventure [perhaps] for a good man some would even dare to die. Romans 5:6-7

Paul became willing to die for everyone, but the sinless Savior had already done that, and He was the only One who could do so without blemish by having never sinned.

Love is the Solution Part One

One of the biggest divisions in our society today is *Pro Choice* at odds with *Pro Life*. Some of the Pro Life backers go far too extreme trying to *force* the Pro Choice advocates to believe what the Pro Life side believes. Instead of approaching the ones who are most in need of caring support with love, they drive the division even further apart—sometimes with violence. Both sides are guilty of going to extremes and intensifying the problem.

Here is how God inspires us to lovingly approach this matter:
> Hereby perceive we the love *of God*, because he laid down his life for us: and we ought to lay down *our* lives for the brethren. 1 John 3:16

The "brethren" refers to all brothers and sisters who are believers in Christ and are adopted children of God the Father. The Lord Jesus goes further saying to love *everyone*:
> But I say to you which hear, Love your enemies, do good to them which hate you. Luke 6:27

We have often heard this plea voiced from the abortion advocates: "*It is the woman's body so it is her freedom of choice.*"

However, we cannot physically hear the choice of the living embryo or fetus saying, "*I would like freedom to continue living and have freedom for pursuit of happiness.*"

Can a fetus speak up when being judged to die? Does anyone care about those who cannot speak for themselves? Our God does:

> [8]Open your mouth for the speechless, in the cause of all who are appointed to die. [9a]Open your mouth, judge righteously. Proverbs 31:8-9a NIV

> Ye shall not respect persons [shall not show partiality] in judgment; *but* ye shall hear the small as well as the great; Deuteronomy 1:17a

One must wonder if the children whose lives were sacrificed to false gods were trying to be heard:

> and the Sepharvites burnt their children in fire to [false gods] Adrammelech and Anammelech, the gods of Sepharvaim. 2 Kings 17:31b

> [36]And they [the Israelites who joined with foreigners] served their idols: which were a snare [a trap] unto them. [37]Yea, they sacrificed their sons and their daughters unto devils [demons], [38]And shed innocent blood, *even* the blood of their sons and daughters, whom they sacrificed unto the idols of Canaan: and the land was polluted with blood. Psalm 106:36-38

Ezekiel 16:20-21; 23:37 repeat the sacrificing of children again as do 2 Kings 17:17, 21:6; and 2 Chronicles 33:6.

As for anyone who's ever been associated with or having taken part in an abortion, they need to be loved, *and* they need to hear the truth. Many abortions have been weakly justified by reason of not wanting the child because of financial hardship or even simply not wanting to take the responsibility. But it is of vital importance to look beyond this temporary life of choices here on earth:

Isaiah the prophet received from God many visions about which to record. Here is one:

> I [our LORD God] have sworn by myself, the word is gone out of my mouth *in* righteousness, and shall not return, That unto me every knee shall bow, every tongue shall swear [take an oath]. Isaiah 45:23

Paul the apostle writes:

> [9]Wherefore God also hath highly exalted him [Jesus], and given him a name which is above every name: [10]That at the name of Jesus every knee should bow, of *things* in heaven, and *things* in earth, and *things* under the earth; [11]And *that* every tongue should confess that Jesus Christ *is* Lord, to the glory of God the Father. Philippians 2:9-11

> So then every one of us shall give account of himself to God. Romans 14:12

Luke, the Gentile physician, quotes Paul saying:

> And I have hope toward God, which they [the Jewish Pharisee high priest, elders, and an orator who were accusing Paul] themselves also allow [accept], that there shall be a resurrection of the dead, both of the just [justified to go to heaven] and the unjust. Acts 24:15

John prophesied the following vision he received from God:

> ^{12}And I saw the dead, small and great, stand before God; and the books were opened: and another book was opened, which is *the book* of life: and the dead were judged out of those things which were written in the books, according to their works. ^{13}And the sea gave up the dead which were in it; and death and hell [the grave called Hādēs] delivered up the dead which were in them: and they were judged every man according to their works. ^{14}And death and hell [Hādēs] were cast into the lake of fire. This is the second death.
> Revelation 20:12-14

Some people take the following verse to mean we are free to disobey. However, the thing from which we are set free is this: we are set free from practicing sin.

> And ye shall know the truth, and the truth shall make you free. John 8:32

> And [Jesus] saying, The time is fulfilled, and the kingdom of God is at hand [near]: repent ye, and believe the gospel. Mark 1:15

> AND IT SHALL COME TO PASS, *THAT* WHOSOEVER SHALL CALL ON THE NAME OF THE LORD SHALL BE SAVED. Acts 2:21

> Behold, now *is* the accepted time; behold, now *is* the day of salvation. 2 Corinthians 6:2b

Harold Summers said of the previous verse, "Now being the accepted time and the day to be saved is important to both the sinner...*and* the *preacher.*" God teaches that all believers are called to serve as *reconcilers* and *ambassadors* for Christ.

> Beloved, let us love one another: for love is of God; and every one that loveth is born of God, and knoweth God. 1 John 4:7

Indoctrination to Commit Fornication

Children as young as five years old and all ages older are being indoctrinated with transsexual and/or *sex education.* The latter is *taught* to ensure their *safety* when engaging in pre-puberty sexual activities. Not only are they being led to believe it is *okay* so long as precautions are taken, but they are *prevented*, in some public schools, from learning the eternal disaster for their souls if they participate.

Immoral Sex

The question needs to be asked, "If there is such a thing as sexual *immorality*, then what is sexual *morality?*" *Immoral sex* will be answered first:

One form of adultery is a man being with another man's wife. God tells us all of His Commandments twice. So we have heard the Seventh Commandment two times:

> Thou shalt not commit adultery. Exodus 20:14; Deuteronomy 5:18

> And the man that committeth adultery with *another* man's wife, *even he* that committeth adultery with his neighbor's wife, the adulterer and the adulteress shall surely be put to death. Leviticus 20:10

Any sexual activity *outside of holy matrimony* between one man and one woman is considered to be adultery. In God's view adultery is *not* being committed if the activity involves only one man and one woman who are truly married as man and wife with God as witness. Without being formally married it is referred to as *fornication* which translates to a form of adultery.

> To fornicate is described as "committing lewdness, as an unmarried man or woman, or as a married man with an unmarried woman." Fornication is further described as "The incontinence or lewdness of unmarried persons, male or female; also, the criminal conversation of a married man with an unmarried woman."[41]

The dictionary touches on, and does not disagree with, what the Lord Jesus says:

> [27]Ye have heard that it was said by them of old time, THOU SHALT NOT COMMIT ADULTERY: [28]But I say unto you, That whosoever looketh on a woman to lust after her hath committed adultery with her already in his heart. Matthew 5:27-28

Even if we look at a picture or a movie with lust in our eyes for what we are seeing, it is considered by our Savior and Judge to be adultery.

Whenever anyone turns that around and is offended by knowing how God will judge us, it is because of "the offense of the cross." Justice and mercy meet at the cross.

Jesus, the Son of God, is the Second Person of God. He knows our thoughts. Even if we have lewd, obscene thoughts, our Creator knows what we are thinking:

⁴And Jesus knowing their thoughts said, Wherefore [why do you] think ye evil in your hearts?"...
²⁵And Jesus knew their thoughts, and said unto them, Every kingdom divided against itself is brought to desolation; and every city or house divided against itself shall not stand; Matthew 9:4; 12:25

But he knew their thoughts, and said to the man which had the withered hand, Rise up, and stand forth in the midst. And he arose and stood forth. Luke 6:8

One may be asking, "Why the reason for discernment on this subject?" The answer is that the married spouses can be so easily tempted by the world's ways to break their promise of faithfulness to each other and to God. The wisdom given in Proverbs informs us:

MY son, attend unto [pay attention to] my wisdom, *and* bow [incline] thine ear to my understanding: ²That thou mayest regard [preserve] discretion, and *that* thy lips may keep knowledge. ³For the lips of a strange [an immoral] woman drop *as* honeycomb [drip honey], and her mouth *is* smoother than oil: ⁴But her end is bitter as wormwood [undrinkable water], sharp as a two-edged sword. ⁵Her feet go down to death; her steps take hold on hell. ⁶Lest thou shouldest ponder the path of life [her life], her ways are movable [unstable], *that* thou canst not know *them.* ⁷Hear me now therefore, O ye children, and depart not from the words of my mouth. ⁸Remove thy way far from her, and come not nigh the door of her house: ⁹Lest thou give thine honor [vigor] unto others, and thy years unto the cruel: ¹⁰Lest strangers be filled with thy wealth [strength]; and thy labors *be* in the house of a stranger [foreigner]; ¹¹And thou mourn at the

last, when thy flesh and thy body are consumed, [12]And say, How have I hated instruction, and my heart despised reproof; [13]And have not obeyed the voice of my teachers, nor inclined mine ear to them that instructed me! [14]I was almost [on the verge of total ruin] in all evil in the midst of the congregation and assembly. ...
[18]Let thy fountain be blessed: and rejoice with the wife of thy youth. [19]*Let her be as* the loving hind [deer] and pleasant roe [graceful doe]; let her breasts satisfy thee at all times; and be thou ravished [be intoxicated] with her love. [20]And why wilt thou, my son, be ravished [enraptured] with a strange [an immoral] woman, and embrace the bosom of a stranger? [21]For the ways of a man *are* before the eyes of the LORD, and he pondereth [observes, weighs] all his goings. Proverbs 5:1-14, 18-21

MY son, keep my words, and lay up [treasure] my commandments with thee. [2]Keep my commandments, and live; and my law as the apple of thine eye. [The Lord Jesus Christ has kept the commandments for you *if* you sincerely repent and ask His forgiveness.] [3]Bind them [His commandments] upon thy fingers, write them upon the table of thine heart. [4]Say unto wisdom, Thou *art* my sister; and call understanding *thy* kinswoman [seductress]: [5]That they may keep thee from the strange [immoral] woman, from the stranger [seductress] *which* flattereth with her words. [6]For at the window of my house I looked through my casement [lattice], [7]And behold among the simple ones, I discerned among the youths, a young man void [devoid] of understanding, [8]Passing through the street near her corner; and he went the way to her house, [9]In the twilight, in the evening, in the black and dark night. [10]And, behold, there met him a woman *with* the attire of a harlot, and subtile [crafty] of heart. [11](She *is* loud and stubborn [rebellious]; her feet abide not in her house: [12]Now *is she* without, now in the streets, and lieth in wait [lurking] at every corner.) [13]So she caught him, and kissed him, *and* with an impudent [defiant or shameless] face said unto him, [14]*I have* peace offerings with me; this day have I paid my vows. [15]Therefore came I forth to meet thee, diligently to seek thy face, and I have found thee. [16]I have decked my bed with coverings of tapestry, with carved *works*, with fine linen of Egypt. [17]I have perfumed my bed with myrrh, aloes, and cinnamon. [18]Come, let us take our fill of love until the morning: let us solace [delight] ourselves with loves. [19]For the Goodman [my husband] *is* not at home, he is gone a long journey. [20]He hath taken a bag of money with him, *and* will come home at the day appointed [at the new or full moon]. [21]With her much fair [enticing] speech she caused him to yield, with the flattering of her lips she forced [seduced] him. [22]He goeth after her straightway [immediately], as an ox goeth to the slaughter, or as a fool to the correction of the stocks [chains]; [23]Till a dart [arrow] strike through his liver; as a bird hasteth to the snare, and knoweth not that it *is* for [would take] his life. [24]Hearken unto me now therefore, O ye children, and attend to the words of my mouth. [25]Let not thine heart decline [turn aside] to her ways, go not astray in her paths. [26]For she hath cast down many wounded: yea, many strong *men* have been slain by her. [27]Her house *is* the way to hell, going down to the chambers of death. Proverbs 7:1-27

Such *is* the way of an adulterous woman; she eateth, and wipeth her mouth, and saith, I have done no wickedness. Proverbs 30:20

These Proverbs, if heeded, add much to the development of discernment. In today's world, there are a multitude of men who are lured in, captivated and seduced by a flirtatious, flattering, adulterous woman.

> Lust not after her beauty in thine heart; neither let her take [allure] thee with her eyelids. Proverbs 6:25

God's Word can save us from temptations. In fact, as difficult as it is to admit, this writer's past proves the wisdom of these Proverbs. Thank God for sending His Son to bring about this life-changing relationship with the Lord Jesus Christ.

We are thankful for the shed blood of Jesus to be the very element that was required to give us forgiveness for our poor decisions and shameful behavior. We only need to swallow our pride and surrender to the fact that only He can save us. By His death taking the place of what would have been our *second death*, and because He lives eternally, believers also have *everlasting life* in Him—with Him—in heaven.

Temptations surround us and necessitate the ability to discern—that is, to make the best choices in each and every situation that confronts us. The moment we first believe, the Holy Spirit indwells us by spiritual baptism. When we are tempted, we simply need to listen to the Spirit in our conscience who can put the Lord Jesus into our hearts and minds; and then the evil departs from us. The last thing Satan wants to see is a praying man, looking to God for help. Satan will flee immediately (James 4:7). With God there is no place for sin to dwell. God separates all sin from Himself.

The Lord Jesus Christ knew no sin; in Him there is no sin; and He committed no sin. He momentarily, on the day He was crucified, took upon Himself the sin of everyone. But now, He is glorified, and He glorified His Father by being obedient to the point of death nailed to the cross; and further glorified

God by trusting His Father to have the Holy Spirit raise Him from the dead on the third day.

The Old Testament Scriptures list the many forms of immoral sex, all of which God prohibits. The Book of Leviticus in chapter 18 names *acts of forbidden immorality*. These include indecent exposure (exposing nakedness); and incest with near of kin, with the father or mother, or the father's wife, sister, daughter, granddaughter, the father's wife's daughter, aunt, uncle, daughter-in-law, sister-in-law, any woman with her daughter. Intercourse was not allowed with a woman during her menstruation. Adultery with another man's wife was forbidden as were the horrifying practices of worshiping the idol called *Molech*, having newborn babies *pass through fire* (Leviticus 18:21). Sodomy or homosexuality was forbidden, as well as sexual activities with an animal. Adultery and idolatry are both brought forth in Leviticus chapter 18 as well as in Leviticus Chapter 20 —which is the chapter that lists the penalties for disobeying God's commands forbidding these acts.

The New Testament also reminds us of these immoral behaviors:

> [18]For the wrath [anger] of God is revealed from heaven against all ungodliness and unrighteousness of men, who hold [suppress] the truth in unrighteousness; [19]Because that which may be known of God is manifest [evident] in [among] them. [20]For the invisible things of him from the creation of the world are clearly seen, being understood by the things that are made, *even* his eternal power and Godhead [divine nature]; so that they are without excuse: [21]Because that, when they knew God, they glorified *him* not as God, neither were thankful; but became vain [futile] in their imaginations [thoughts], and their foolish heart was darkened. [22]Professing themselves to be wise, they became fools, [23]And changed the glory of the uncorruptible God into an image made like

to corruptible [perishable] man, and to birds, and four-footed beasts, and creeping things. [24]Wherefore God also gave them up to uncleanness through the lusts of their own hearts, to dishonor their own bodies between themselves. [25]Who changed [exchanged] the truth of God into [for the lie] a lie, and worshiped and served the creature more [rather] than the Creator, who is blessed for ever. Amen. [26]For this cause God gave them up unto vile affections: for even their women did change [exchange] the natural use into [for] that which is against nature: [27]And likewise also the men [males], leaving the natural use of the woman [female], burned in their lust one toward another; men with men working that which is unseemly [shameful], and receiving in themselves that recompense [penalty] of their error which was meet [due]. [28]And even as they did not like to retain God in *their* knowledge, God gave them over to a reprobate [debased, no foundation for sound reasoning] mind, to do those things which are not convenient [fitting]; [29]Being filled with all unrighteousness, fornication, wickedness, covetousness, maliciousness; full of envy, murder, debate [strife], deceit, malignity [evil mindedness]; whisperers, [30]Backbiters, haters of God, despiteful [violent], proud, boasters, inventors of evil things, disobedient to parents, [31]Without understanding, covenantbreakers [promise breakers], without natural affection, implacable [unforgiving], unmerciful: [32]Who knowing the [righteous judgment] judgment of God, that they which commit such things are worthy of death, not only do the same, but have pleasure in [approve of] them that do them. Romans 1:18-32

That long list of disobedient acts against God and his created people needs to be of utmost importance to, as verse 32
states, even those who approve of such acts. Why? Because
the penalty is death—the *second death* which is the final wrath
of God's judgment by casting the unrepentant into the eternal,
non-quenchable Lake of Fire.

The Lord Jesus tells us that the ones who will come to believe during the Tribulation will be subjected to the hatred by
those mentioned in Romans 1:18-32.

> [9]Then shall they deliver you up to be afflicted [to trib-
> ulation], and shall kill you: and ye shall be hated of all
> nations for my name's sake. [10]And then shall many be
> offended, and shall betray one another, and shall hate
> one another. [11]And many false prophets shall rise, and
> shall deceive many. [12]And because iniquity [lawless-
> ness] shall abound, the love of many shall wax [grow]
> cold. [13]But he that shall endure unto the end, the same
> shall be saved. Matthew 24:9-13

Paul the apostle tells of the eternal danger for practicing
what offends God:

> [9]Know ye not that the unrighteous shall not inherit the
> kingdom of God? Be not deceived: neither fornicators
> [the sexually immoral], nor idolators, nor adulterers, nor
> effeminate [homosexuals], nor abusers of themselves
> [sodomites] with mankind, [10]Nor thieves, nor covetous,
> nor drunkards, nor revilers, nor extortioners, shall in-
> herit the kingdom of God. 1 Corinthians 6:9-10

There is a stern warning given to those who promote or
indoctrinate the otherwise innocent children in these sexually

oriented matters. The Son of God, Jesus Christ, gives the warning in the three Gospel Books of Matthew, Mark, and Luke:

> [6]But whoso shall offend [cause to sin] one of these little ones which believe in me, it were better for him that a millstone were hanged about his neck, and *that* he were drowned in the depth of the sea. [7]Woe unto the world because of offenses [enticement to sin]! For it must needs be that offenses come; but woe to that man by whom the offense cometh! Matthew 18:6-7; (Mark 9:42; Luke 17:1-2)

God does not want us to become lost in all the other goings-on. God wants marriages to last—He hates divorce. However, the Lord Jesus makes it clear that if a spouse commits adultery, then a divorce is justified:

> But I say unto you, That whosoever shall put away [divorce] his wife, saving [except] for the cause of fornication [sexual immorality], causeth her to commit adultery: and whosoever shall marry her that is divorced committeth adultery. Matthew 5:32

Sex with Morality

Now to answer the question, when is engaging in sex considered to be *moral*?

In some homes, the word *sex* has become a *dirty word*, probably because the whole counsel of God—that is, the entirety of Scripture on the subject of sex most likely has not been included. If only the previous description about *immoral sex* is considered then, of course *sex* becomes a *repulsive subject*. However, God created man and woman the way He designed them for His own good reasons. And when we exercise His design, *everything* needs to be done the way God's Word prescribes. *Everything* includes marriage:

> And the LORD God said, *It is* not good that the man should be alone; I will make him a helper meet [helper comparable to him] for him. Genesis 2:18

The following verses establish the marriage and its consummation between one man and one woman:

> Therefore shall a man leave his father and his mother, and shall cleave [be joined] unto his wife: and they shall be one flesh. Genesis 2:24

When God created human beings, He created them *male* and *female* in order for them to be procreative in bringing forth more human beings:

> [27]So God created man in His *own* image; in the image of God created he him; male and female created he them. [28a]And God blessed them, and God said unto them, Be fruitful and multiply...
> [31a]And God saw everything that he had made, and, behold, *it was* very good. Genesis 1:27-28a, 31a

Since God told them to *multiply*, He obviously intended for the married couple to be attracted to each other and to engage in moral sex ...and not to be confused...not to think that the act they would be doing would make them guilty of immoral, sexual sin.

> Male and female created he them; and blessed them, and called their name Adam [Mankind] in the day they were created. Genesis 5:2

He created neither transgender, nor doubt, nor *confusion*.
For God is not *the author* of confusion but of peace.
1 Corinthians 14:33a

Paul the apostle wrote to the Corinthians recommending the following:

> Nevertheless, *to avoid* fornication, let every man have his own wife, and let every woman have her own husband. 1 Corinthians 7:2

That verse confirms that marriage is for one male with one female. For each *man to have his own wife* also means monogamous marriage. This verse echoes and reinforces the principle that God's order for His own people is that a person should have only one spouse. And the spouse is to be of the opposite biological gender.

Marriage is God's *only* provision for sexual fulfillment. *However*, marriage should not be reduced simply to overly indulging to satisfy that desire.

> [3]Let the husband render unto the wife due benevolence [affection]: and likewise also the wife unto the husband. [4]The wife hath not power of [authority over] her own body, but the husband: and likewise also the husband hath not power of his own body, but the wife. [5]Defraud [Deprive] ye not the other except *it be* with consent for a time, that ye may give yourselves to fasting and prayer; and come together again [sexual affection with the spouse] that Satan tempt you not for your incontinency [because of lack of self-control].
> 1 Corinthians 7:3-5

Note the delicacy Paul uses on this topic. How respectful the mutual affection of the spouses. There is no crudeness or vulgarity. How different from the world!

In the context of this passage, to honor and respect the spouse's lack of desire at some times, patience and compassionate understanding should be offered.

The cautions in these verses are to remind us that Satan is always quick to take advantage of any weakness. If a faithful spouse is even given over to *thoughts* that are vulgar, it becomes *fornication* and is considered adultery in the heart. Spouses need to support each other to defeat Satan in this natural battle. They should beat the devil at his own game:

> [33]But he that is married careth for the things that are of the world, how he may please *his* wife....
>
> [34b]but she that is married careth for the things of the world, how she may please *her* husband.
>
> 1 Corinthians 7:33, 34b

God wants us to be pleasing to our spouses, and, in our daily walk, to first be spiritually pleasing to Him, too:

> that you may walk worthy of the Lord, fully pleasing *Him*... Colossians 1:10a. NIV

Making the commitment *to fasting and prayer* means we're to devote the greater amount of time to the Lord's desires for when we're not devoting ourselves to the short time of fulfilling our spouse's desires. Since God knows our thoughts, we can, many times throughout the day, pray in our thoughts, even while we're driving, working, or having a conversation with others.

God created male and female hormones for sexual drive, so, God firmly tells Christian couples we're *not to deprive* our partner's rights for *too long a period of time* so that *lack of self-control* will not yield to the world's temptations. Why? Because *after* an *agreed upon time* of abstinence, sexual desires can intensify and a spouse can become more vulnerable to sinful temptations. This is *part of* the reason married believers are not to sexually deprive their spouses.

God wants us to understand His intention—His context—His full counsel. He wants us to remember we are *in* the world, not *of* the world. He wants nearly 100% of our time to be devoted to Him. When we are focused upon Him—again, it's called *fasting and praying*. God wants us to be in fellowship with Him *often*—not *seldom*—so that He will be the center of our focus and attention.

The Bible describes the Lord Jesus Christ being the Husband of His bride, the Church. The Church is made up of all universal believers in Almighty God. John the apostle writes of the vision of the future raptured Church to heaven:

> [7]Let us be glad and rejoice, and give honor [glory] to him: for the marriage of the Lamb [Jesus] is come, and his wife [the Church of believers] hath made herself ready. [8]And to her was granted that she should be arrayed in fine linen, clean and white [bright]: for the fine linen is the righteousness [righteous acts] of saints [The believers are viewed by the Father as being righteous simply because they believe.]. [9]And he saith unto me, Write, Blessed *are* they which are called unto the marriage supper of the Lamb. And he saith unto me, These are the true sayings of God. Revelation 19:7-9

The Church in heaven will be praising the Lord Jesus for all eternity for bringing them back from having been separated from God:

And they sung a new song, saying, Thou art worthy to take the book [scroll], and to open the seals thereof: for thou wast slain [crucified], and hast redeemed us to God by thy blood out of every kindred [tribe], and tongue [language], and people, and nation; Revelation 5:9

Paul the apostle explains how, while still here on this earth, we're to also *often* remember what the Lord Jesus did for us when He shed His blood and died on the cross. In verses 24 and 25 below, Paul quotes what Jesus said on the eve of His death. Take note in verses 25 and 26 that we compare this coming together *often* in sweet fellowship with the coming together *often* of the husband and wife in their marriage relationship:

[23]For I have received of the Lord that which also I delivered unto you, That the Lord Jesus the *same* night in which he was betrayed took bread: [24]And when he had given thanks, he brake [broke] *it*, and said, Take, eat: this is my body, which is broken for you: this do in remembrance of me. [25]After the same manner also *he took* the cup, when he had supped [after supper], saying, This cup is the new testament in my blood: this do ye, as oft [often] as ye drink *it*, in remembrance of me. [26]For as often as ye eat this bread, and drink this cup, ye do show [proclaim] the Lord's death till he come.
1 Corinthians 11:23-26

Just as it's important for the family to often come to supper together, it is important to often come to the Lord's Supper— and it is important for the husband and wife to often be affectionate with each other. Due to Christ being resurrected on the first day of the week, and the Church's beginning fifty days later at Pentecost—on the first day of the week—the early church soon established the tradition of coming together for the Lord's Supper on each and every *first day of the week*.

> And upon the first *day* of the week, when the disciples came together to break bread... Acts 20:7a

Paul commands believers to keep the traditions:

> Keep the ordinances [traditions], as I delivered *them* to you. 1 Corinthians 11:2b

When we are in fellowship with the Lord's Supper the outside world ceases to exist—we're totally focused on our Lord and Savior, caught up in the Spirit. But prior to the meeting, we are to examine ourselves and ask forgiveness of any sin. We only approach this meeting with a clear conscience and a clean heart. Believers do this in order to be in fellowship with the sinless Lord Jesus Christ and with the other believers who have also been cleansed of their unrighteousness.

> BEHOLD, how good and how pleasant *it is* for brethren to dwell together in unity! Psalm 133:1

Likewise, as long as neither spouse has been defiled, God tells man and wife to *come together* again—just as He tells us in Hebrews 10:25 to not forsake the assembling of ourselves *together*...in the assembly meeting on the 1st day of the week. The reason for the meeting is for the breaking of bread time, fellowship time, prayer time, and teaching time (Acts 2:42). He is even further pleased when we have Bible studies during midweek, and when we spend our quiet, personal prayer time—all in fellowship with our God and with each other. Nothing on this earth is more important. Our citizenship is in heaven.

We share a genuine desire to please our God and to be pleased by His blessings. Similarly the married couple shares a genuine desire to please each other and to be pleased in return. As the husband and wife are allowed to give total attention to each other, the outside world is not in their thoughts. The world seems to cease to exist. Simply pleasing our spouse is in our thoughts when we please each other with loving affection.

> God addresses human sexuality from a *holistic* perspective of His intention and design. In contrast to modern day increasingly compelling obsession with sex, the Bible places sex within the total context of human nature, happiness, and holiness.[42]

As we fast [hold fast/stand fast] and pray, only pleasing God is what is in our thoughts, and He fervently desires this fellowship with us—as we do with Him.

Since this is a huge part of God's divine intention, neither spouse should deprive the other of the obligations of married life.

Christian married couples don't want their private relationship activities publicly made known. It's nobody else's business. For the married this is a deeply personal, intimate sharing of affection which is kept discreet within the marriage relationship. What a far cry from the LGBTQ+ and gay pride parades and demonstrations.

The obvious reason this in-depth explanation is in the Bible is because God saw this coming. Perhaps depriving could be a reaction to the gross sexual immorality we read of in Romans chapter one and First Corinthians chapter six. Or possibly deprivation could be due to guilty feelings of our own wretch-filled past. God's Word and His forgiveness free our minds of any such idea.

God and Satan are at war; God knows our nature to sin, even in thoughts with this inner on-going battle.

No one could ever give the amount of love, patience, and forgiveness for any of our *disgusting acts* as our God and Savior has given.

It is with sincere love and compassion for the father, mother, and child, that this life changing relationship with the Lord Jesus Christ be accepted. That which He offers results in *hope* of eternal life together.

The Hope

Even those who are responsible for the sin of indoctrinating little children to commit fornication can have hope to see the kingdom of heaven...*if* only they accept God's free offer and sincerely repent and ask God to forgive them. The only unforgivable sin today is rejecting our God and Savior. Only by the work of Christ nailed onto the cross can hope be achieved.

> Behold the Lamb of God, which taketh away the sin of the world. John 1:29b

> For God sent not his Son into the world to condemn the world; but that the world through him might be saved. John 3:17

> [12]Then shall ye call upon me, and ye shall go and pray unto me, and I will hearken unto [listen to] you. [13]And ye shall seek me, and find *me*, when ye shall search for me with all your heart. Jeremiah 29:12-13

> behold, now *is* the accepted time; behold, now *is* the day of salvation. 2 Corinthians 6:2b

The greatest hope we have during this temporary life on earth is to know our spirits and souls continue in the eternal realm when we die and to know that when we are raptured to heaven, we will be given *new bodies*!

> [20]For our conversation [citizenship] is in heaven; from whence also we look for the Savior, the Lord Jesus Christ: [21]Who shall change our vile body, that it may be fashioned like unto his glorious body, according to the working whereby he is able even to subdue all things unto himself. Philippians 3:20-21

Although the ones who teach others to become sinners can be saved, they might not receive further reward. But at least they can all eventually end up in heaven. The Lord Jesus explains it best:

> Whosoever therefore shall break one of these least commandments, and shall teach men so, he shall be called the least in the kingdom of heaven: but whosoever shall do and teach *them*, the same shall be called great in the kingdom of heaven. Matthew 5:19

The above verse, Matthew 5:19, means that a person, even though a believer, who breaks the Law, and teaches others to also break the Law (*set free* "to disobey"), will be the least in heaven. The second part of the verse tells of the believer who *practices* and *teaches* obedience. The Ten Commandments do not save us. Rather, the Law makes us knowledgeable that we have sinned and that we are in need of the Savior.

Paul the apostle also explains:

> [13]Every [believing] man's [and woman's] work shall be made manifest [will become evident to God]: for the day shall declare it, because it shall be revealed by fire;

and the fire shall try [test] every man's work of what sort it is. [14]If any man's work abide [endures] which he hath built thereupon, he shall receive a reward. [15]If any man's work shall be burned, he shall suffer loss: but he himself shall be saved; yet so as by [through] fire.
1 Corinthians 3:13-15

But a person who teaches the truth of the Scriptures and practices what he preaches will be rewarded for being a good and faithful servant of God. The Savior gives an example of that in the closing of a parable:

His lord said unto him, Well done, good and faithful servant; thou hast been faithful over a few things, I will make thee ruler over many things, enter thou into the joy of thy lord. Matthew 25:23

Love is the Solution Part Two

Love is such an important issue, there needs to be more emphasis with repetition. The word *love* is in the Bible over three hundred times. A true believing Christian realizes there are no errors in the Scriptures. The *professed* Christian who even verbally attacks LGBTQ+ or abortionists obviously has not heard or has not understood Christ's teaching on the subject of loving one another.

The reason believers at least try to obey the commandments is because this is the way a person can express his love for having been loved. Jesus is quoted:

If ye love me, keep my commandments. John 14:15

He that hath my commandments, and keepeth them, he it is that loveth me: and he that loveth me shall be loved of my Father, and I will love him, and will mani-fest [reveal] myself to him. John 14:21

For this is the [our] love of God, that we keep his com-mandments: and his commandments are not grievous [are not burdensome]. 1 John 5:3

One of the main reasons we not only obey Him, but also truly do love Him, since *love is the solution*, bears repeating. This is because of the answer Jesus gave to the Pharisee scribe who asked Him which of the commandments was the most important:

[28]And one of the scribes came, and having heard them reasoning together, and perceiving that he had an-swered them well, asked him, Which is the first [fore-most] commandment of all? [29]And Jesus answered him, The first [foremost] of all the commandments *is*, HEAR, O ISRAEL; THE LORD OUR GOD IS ONE LORD. [30]AND THOU SHALT LOVE THE LORD THY GOD WITH ALL THY HEART, AND WITH ALL THY SOUL, AND WITH ALL THY MIND, AND WITH ALL THY STRENGTH: THIS IS THE FIRST COMMANDMENT. [31]And the second *is* like, *namely* this, THOU SHALT LOVE THY NEIGH-BOR AS THYSELF. There is none other commandment greater than these. Mark 12:28-31

The second, *Thou shalt love thy neighbor as thyself*, is the most repeated verse in the New Testament from the Old Tes-tament. It is basically the traditional *Golden Rule*. It originated in Leviticus:

Thou shalt not avenge [take vengeance], nor bear any grudge against the children of thy people, but thou shalt love thy neighbor as thyself: I *am* the LORD. Leviticus 19:18

Why do professed Christians appear to hold *a grudge* against a homosexual person? God loves all of us, and He died on the cross for all of us. We are all miraculously created by God.

> For God so loved [all] the [people of] the world, that he gave his only begotten Son... John 3:16a

The *Golden Rule* is stated in Matthew and Luke, and in both Jesus is quoted:

> Therefore all things whatsoever ye would that men should do to you, do ye even so to them: for this is the law and the prophets. Matthew 7:12

> And as ye would that men should do to you, do ye also to them likewise. Luke 6:31

The Golden Rule has been restated in other wording to make it understandable for other English speaking people: "Do unto others as you would have others do unto you." This author's mother used to say, "Treat everyone like they won't be here tomorrow."

Following is the continuation of New Testament verses that repeat the original in Leviticus 19:18:

> THOU SHALT LOVE THY NEIGHBOR AS THYSELF. Matthew 19:19b; Matthew 22:39B; Mark 12:31b; Luke 10:27b, d; Romans 13:9b; Galatians 5:14b; James 2:8b

Who is your *NEIGHBOR*? Your neighbor is anyone who is in need of something you have and that he does not have. The believer has eternal life: Never forget John 3:16 and be ready to share what you have. If he asks you, love him and tell him the truth:

> That whosoever believes in him should not perish, but have everlasting life. John 3:16b

> *Be* ready always to *give* an answer [a defense] to every man that asketh you a reason of the hope that is in you with meekness and fear [reverential awe]. 1 Peter 3:15b

In order to share this *everlasting life* with anyone else who does not have it, the believer needs to approach, not with accusations; rather with gentleness and respect:

> *Let* nothing *be done* through strife or vainglory [empty pride]; but in lowliness of mind let each esteem other better than themselves. Philippians 2:3

> Honor all men. 1 Peter 2:17a

True peace comes by loving one another and by minds thinking alike.

> For this is the message that ye heard from the beginning, that we should love one another. 1 John 3:11

> Hereby perceive we the love *of God,* because he laid down his life for us: and we ought to lay down *our* lives for the brethren [our brothers and sisters in Christ]. 1 John 3:16

> My little children [the younger disciples whom the elder John is teaching], let us not love in word, neither in tongue; but in deed and in truth. 1 John 3:18

[7]Beloved, let us love one another: for love is of God; and every one that loveth is born of God, and knoweth God. [8]He that loveth not knoweth not God; for God is love. [9]In this was manifested [revealed] the love of God toward us, because that God sent his only begotten Son into the world, that we might live through him. [10]Herein is love, not that we loved God, but that he loved us, and sent his Son *to be* the propitiation [the blood that Christ shed for believers to be forgiven, and their faith in it that satisfies the Father's righteous, justified anger] for our sins. [11]Beloved, if God so loved us, we ought also to love one another. 1 John 4:7-11

We love him, because he first loved us. 1 John 4:19

But God commendeth his love toward us, in that, while we were yet sinners, Christ died for us. Romans 5:8

[12]Put on therefore, as the elect [chosen only due to our believing] of God, holy and beloved, bowels of mercies [tender mercies], kindness, humbleness of mind, meekness, long-suffering [patience]; [13]Forbearing [Bearing with] one another, and forgiving one another, if any man have a quarrel against any: even as Christ forgave you, so also *do* ye. [14]And above all these things *put on* charity [love], which is the bond of perfectness. Colossians 3:12-14

And now abideth faith, hope, charity [love], these three; but the greatest of these *is* charity [love]. 1 Corinthians 13:13

Being likeminded in the same love as God has shown us and everyone else who lives by the same standard—that is, all going *according to the sound doctrine* of God's Word—results in *peace* with one another...and *love* for one another:

> Fulfill ye my joy, that ye be likeminded, having the same love, *being* of one accord, of one mind. Philippians 2:2

> Be of good comfort, be of one mind, live in peace, and the God of love and peace shall be with you.
> 2 Corinthians 13:11b

> Let us walk by the same rule, let us mind the same thing [be of the same mind]. Philippians 3:16b

> *Be* of the same mind one toward another...
> Romans 12:16

> Now the God of patience and consolation [comfort] grant you to be likeminded one toward another according to Christ Jesus. Romans 15:5

> To be spiritually minded *is* life and peace. Romans 8:6b

> [38]For I am persuaded, that neither death, nor life, nor angels, nor principalities, nor powers, nor things present, nor things to come, [39]Nor height, nor depth, nor any other creature, shall be able to separate us from the love of God, which is in Christ Jesus our Lord.
> Romans 8:38-39

Believers are taught to not get into arguments about what the Bible says. Disputes cause conflicts that only result in strife and a competition to see who can be superior to the other to win the debate.

> But avoid foolish questions [disputes], and genealogies, and contentions, and strivings about the law; for they are unprofitable and vain [useless]. Titus 3:9

Having the capability to discern the Scriptures—an ability given by the Holy Spirit upon believing in God—will definitely result in huge benefits during our eternal futures. When the human mind absorbs and digests the written Word, God's awesome greatness and loving kindness produce within us a love in return, and the hope we have for everlasting life with all those who are likeminded.

Chapter 7

Discernment and its Consequences

This chapter will begin with a look again at what prevents a man from having the ability to develop discernment, will progress to the consequences of either obtaining discernment or not, and will end with some amazing prophecies that have been fulfilled and that can stir the heart to hunger for more of God's truth.

In order to function with good reasoning ability the human mind must be grounded upon a stable foundation. And, in order to understand Scripture, a person must be indwelt by the One who inspired the Bible's remarks and declarations. There has to be a base upon which the intellect can have a starting point:

All Scripture *is* given by inspiration of God.
2 Timothy 3:16a

[16]That he [God] would grant you, according to the riches of his glory, to be strengthened with might by his Spirit in the inner man; [17]That Christ may dwell in your hearts by faith; that ye, being rooted and grounded in

love, [18]May be able to comprehend [understand] with all saints [all other believers] what *is* the breath, and length, and depth, and height; [19]And to know the love of Christ, which passeth knowledge , that ye might be filled with the fullness of God. Ephesians 3:16-19

The holy scriptures...are able to make thee wise unto salvation through faith which is in Christ Jesus.
2 Timothy 3:15b

If a man does not have faith, trust, and belief in Christ, then he cannot know the things of God, because they are spiritually discerned.

But the natural man [the unbelieving man] receiveth not the things of the Spirit of God: for they are foolishness unto him: neither can he know *them* [God's intentions], because they are spiritually discerned.
1 Corinthians 2:14

That verse certainly intensifies the vital necessity of developing discernment. The most important decision a person can make during this temporary life on earth is the choice to adhere to the fact of God's truth in that Jesus Christ the Lord is the only way to heaven.

Jesus saith unto him [Thomas], I am the way, the truth, and the life: no man cometh unto the Father, but by me. John 14:6

First to be addressed are the verses in which God gives people their own way if they so choose and allows them to use their freedom to please themselves with shameful behavior—where He gives them over to a debased mind—a mind with no base—no foundation—a lacking of reasoning ability, making poor decisions—a mind not grounded in His ways, but in immoral, despicable conduct. While reading the following passage, we must remember, not one of us is perfect. We've all broken at least one Commandment, God led Paul to prophesy what we see going on in today's world:

[22]Professing themselves to be wise, they became fools, [23]And changed the glory of the uncorruptible God into an image made like to corruptible [perishable] man, and to birds, and four-footed beasts, and [notice the downward spiral] creeping things. [24]Wherefore God also gave them up to uncleanness through the lusts of their own hearts, to dishonor their own bodies between themselves. [25]Who changed the truth of God into a lie, and worshiped and served the creature more than the Creator, who is blessed for ever. Amen. [26]For this cause God gave them up unto vile affections: for even their women did change the natural use into that which is against nature: [27]And likewise also the men [males] leaving the natural use of the woman [female], burned in their lust one toward another; men with men working that which is unseemly [shameful], and receiving in themselves that recompense [penalty] of their error which was meet [due]. [28]And even as they did not like to retain God in *their* knowledge, God gave them over to a reprobate [debased, no foundation for reasoning] mind, to do things which are not convenient [not fitting]; [29]"Being filled with all unrighteousness, fornication, wickedness, covetousness, maliciousness; full of envy, murder, debate, malignity; whisperers, [30]Backbiters, haters of God, despiteful [violent], proud, boasters, inventors of evil things, disobedient to parents, [31]Without understanding, covenantbreakers, without natural affection, implacable [unforgiving], unmerciful: [32]Who knowing the

judgment [righteous judgment] of God, that they which commit such things are worthy of death, not only do the same, but have pleasure in [approve of] them that do them. Romans 1:22-32

True believer Christians are not to judge the above offenses. This judging is left up to God. For believers are to love them and should be reminded that they too, have all committed sins:

> [3]For we ourselves also were sometimes foolish, disobedient, deceived, serving divers [diverse] lusts and pleasures, living in malice and envy, hateful, *and* hating one another. [4]But after that the kindness and love of God our Savior toward man appeared, [5]Not by works of righteousness which we have done, but according to his mercy he saved us, and renewing of the Holy Ghost; [6]Which he shed on us abundantly through Jesus Christ our Savior; [7]That being justified by his grace, we should be made heirs according to the hope of eternal life. [8]*This* is a faithful saying, and these things I will [want] that thou affirm constantly, that they which have believed in God might be careful to maintain good works. These things are good and profitable unto men.
> Titus 3:3-8

A question has been asked by the evolutionists, "Which came first, the chicken or the egg?" If the egg came first, then, where did it come from? Or better yet, how will the egg prove to be viable if there is no hen to keep it at its critical temperature to be hatched?

Using discernment the logical answer is that for procreation there must be a male and a female. The chickens—that is, the rooster *and* the hen—both had to be created first. Of course, a hen can lay an egg without a rooster, but then there would be no offspring. The egg would only be good for eating, not for reproducing. Therefore, like all of God's creatures, He created them *male* and *female.*

> [26]And God said, Let us [notice the plurality with the pronoun *us*; God: the Father, Christ, and the Holy Spirit were all there for the creating.] make man in our image [sinless at the time He created us], after our likeness: and let them have dominion over the fish of the sea, and over the fowl of the air, and over the cattle, and over all the earth, and over every creeping thing that creepeth upon the earth. [27]So God created man in his *own* image, in the image of God created he him; male and female created he them. Genesis 1:26-27
>
> Male and female created he them; and blessed them, and called their name Adam [Mankind], in the day when they were created. Genesis 5:2

Not only did God create them, of all varieties, male and female, He also made the different species to be of *one kind.* In chapter 1 of Genesis, *after his* or *after their* kind is repeated *ten* times. Plants, fish, animals, fowls, humans—all were created in the adult stages of life to begin the life cycle of each *kind.* A dog cannot produce offspring with a cat. A horse cannot do so with a cow. If we plant an apple tree it cannot bring oranges; it can only produce its own *kind*; like for example: pears, by grafting pear limbs onto the branches.

> And God said, Let the earth bring forth grass, the herb yielding seed, *and* the fruit tree yielding fruit after his kind, whose seed *is* in itself, upon the earth: and it was so. Genesis 1:11

And the earth brought forth grass, *and* herb yielding seed after his kind, and the tree yielding fruit, whose seed *was* in itself, after his kind: and God saw that *it was* good." Genesis 1:12

And God created great whales, and every living creature that moveth, which the waters brought forth abundantly, after their kind, and every winged fowl after his kind: and God saw that *it was* good. Genesis 1:21

And God said, Let the earth bring forth the living creature after his kind, cattle, and creeping thing, and beast of the earth after his kind: and it was so. Genesis 1:24

And God made the beast of the earth after his kind, and cattle after their kind, and every thing that creepeth upon the earth after his kind: and God saw that *it was* good. Genesis 1:25

When God creates a human *being*—a number of months before the *being* is born—He has created a masterpiece—a living creature—and He is willing to save him.

I will praise thee; for I am fearfully *and* wonderfully made... Psalm 139:14a

[24]Thus saith the LORD, thy redeemer, and he that formed thee from the womb, I *am* the LORD that maketh all *things*; that stretcheth [out] forth the heavens [the stars, planets, galaxies, etc.] alone [all alone]; that spreadeth abroad the earth by myself; [25]That frustrateth the tokens of the liars [signs of the babblers], and maketh [drives] diviners mad; that turneth wise *men* backward, and maketh their knowledge foolish; Isaiah 44:24-25

When God created this author and the person who is reading this, He created us in our mothers' wombs, and we are extensions of God's plan for the earth to be populated:

The first man, Adam, and the first woman, Eve, were created as *full grown adults*. When all plants and trees and grasses were first created, they were already at *full growth*. These all happened during the first week—during God's creative week of miracles by His perfect spoken *word*: "Let there be light" (Genesis 1:3) "Let there be firmament" (Genesis 1:6). Quoting Warren Henderson's first volume of his Old Testament commentary:

> "God could have just thought creation into existence, or spoken it into being with one word, but He chose to declare creation order, that we might understand His purposes. Before there was creation, there was communication. God is an articulating God who wants us to comprehend what He reveals to us (Deut. 29:29). We understand by faith, that creation was spoken into existence (Ps. 33:6-10; Heb. 11:3)."[43]

> [27]So God created man in his *own* image, in the image of God created he him; male and female created he them. [28]And God blessed them, and God said unto them, Be fruitful, and multiply, and replenish [fill] the earth, and subdue it: and have dominion over the fish of the sea, and over the fowl of the air, and over every living thing that moveth on the earth. Genesis 1:27-28

For hundreds of years many people have expressed doubt about the entire earth being flooded.

> However, in recent years, their argument is being squelched by the fact that fish fossils have been found on Mt. Everest.[44]

AND God blessed Noah and his sons, and said unto them, Be fruitful, and multiply, and replenish [fill] the earth. ... [7]And you, be ye fruitful, and multiply; bring forth abundantly in the earth, and multiply therein. Genesis 9:1, 7

"From Adam's beginning at 4,004 years before the incarnate birth of Christ, the people were multiplied for 1,656 years."[45]

Then, due to their *wickedness* (Is not wickedness abounding in our nations today?); God destroyed them with the Flood:

AND it came to pass, when men began to multiply on the face of the earth, and daughters were born unto them, ...

[5]And God saw that the wickedness of man *was* great in the earth, and *that* every imagination [intent] of the thoughts of his heart *was* only evil continually [all the day]. [6]And it repented [the LORD was sorry] the LORD that he had made man on the earth, and it grieved him at his heart. [7]And the LORD said, I will destroy man whom I have created from the face of the earth; Genesis 6:1, 5-7a

Only eight people were left to multiply the population for the next nearly 5,000 years: These eight were Noah and his wife and their three sons, Japeth, Shem, Ham, and their three wives. Since that time, over fifty nations have been born—with a world population of over six billion people. Now the wickedness is again grieving our Creator, and He does not conceal the fact that He is again going to destroy it all:

[10]But the day of the Lord will come as a thief [robber] in the night; in the which the heavens shall pass away

with a great noise, and the elements shall melt with fervent heat, the earth also and the works that are therein shall be burned up. [11]*Seeing* then *that* all these shall be dissolved, what manner *of persons* ought ye to be in *all* holy conversation [conduct] and godliness, [12]Looking for and hasting [hastening] unto the coming of the day of God, wherein the heavens being on fire shall be dissolved, and the elements shall melt with fervent heat? [13]Nevertheless we, according to his promise, look for new heavens and a new earth, wherein dwelleth righteousness. [14]Wherefore, beloved, seeing that ye look for such things, be diligent that ye may be found of him in peace, without spot, and blameless. 2 Peter 3:10-14

As Jabe Nicholson said, "The world did not come in with a *big bang*, but it will certainly go out with a 'big bang'!"

All people whom God has created—even those who died in the flood and those who have come since—will face the Lord Jesus to be judged either for eternal life in heaven, or else for eternal suffering in the Lake of Fire. There is no in-between. God will never let go, not one way or any other.

[7]He that overcometh shall inherit all things [all things includes heaven]; and I will be his God, and he shall be my son. [8]But the fearful [cowardly], and unbelieving, and the abominable, and murderers, and whoremongers [sexually immoral], and sorcerers, and idolaters, and all liars, shall have their part in the lake which burneth with fire and brimstone: which is the second death. Revelation 21:7-8

With that Revelation passage, the title statement of *Developing Discernment* chapter 2 is reaffirmed: The decision to accept or reject is truly a matter of life or death.

Prophets, Prophecy, and Prophesy

With all the lawlessness, chaos, rioting, looting, turmoil, immorality, murders, more frequent earthquakes, hurricanes, wildfires, and nuclear build-ups going on in the world today, it all prompts one to sense the nearness of the end times as being absolutely imminent. The prophets of the Bible have much to reveal relating to this matter as they have accurately presented God's perfection in these foretellings.

The word *prophet* can mean either one of two things: 1) A prophet *was* a person who was told by God directly, to foretell God's future events. 2) A prophet *is* a person who brings forth (preaches) God's truth from His Words in the Bible. In both the Old and New Testament Scriptures, prophets were called by God to see or hear His upcoming things to take place, and to declare God's truths. The prophecies of the future have all been included in the Bible; therefore, *today's* prophets are called by God to only bring forth God's Word. True prophets have been described as "the mouthpieces of the true God."

> James Strong describes: "a true prophet to be a person who speaks God's message to the people, under the influence [leading or inspiration] of the divine Spirit." Hence, in general 'the prophet' was one upon whom the Spirit of God rested.[46]

The words *prophecy* and *prophesy* both have to do with telling what God has inspired, but *prophecy* is a noun, and *prophesy* is a verb.

The word *prophecy*, with the last two letters *cy*, is pronounced like *see* at the end—prof-e-*see*. It is a noun which means a *foretelling*.

> "It [a prophecy] is a prediction, or a declaration of something to come. As God only knows future events with certainy, no being but God or some person informed by Him, can utter a real *prophecy*."[47]

> "In general, 'the prophet' was one upon whom the Spirit of God rested, Numbers 11:17-29, one, to whom and through whom God speaks, Numbers 12:2; Amos 3:7, 8."[48]

God inspired Moses to write what He had said to him:

> And he [God] said, Hear now my words: If there be a prophet among you, *I* the LORD will make myself known unto him in a vision, *and* will speak unto him in a dream. Numbers 12:6

The reason the prophecies were written in past tense was because God told the prophets who foretold the future events what to write by giving them a vision or a dream. The prophets were writing what they had seen in a vision or a dream.

> [20]Knowing this first, that no prophecy of the scripture is of any private interpretation [origin]. [21]For the prophecy came not in old [any] time by the will of man: but holy men of God spake *as they were* moved by the Holy Ghost. 2 Peter 1:20-21

> "The prophecies recorded in Scriptures, as those who uttered the *prophecies* could not have foreknown the events predicted without supernatural instruction."[49]

The word *prophesy,* with the last two letters *sy,* is pronounced like *sigh*—prof-e-*sigh*, and it is a verb. It can refer to foretelling the future *or* to bringing forth what is already written in Scripture:

> To prophesy can also mean: "To interpret or explain Scripture."[50]

Most prophets in the Bible were men, but there were also some women who were prompted by God, such as Miriam, Deborah, Huldah, Anna, and the four daughters of Philip the evangelist. (Exodus15:20; Judges 4:4; Kings 22:14; Luke 2:36; Acts 21:9). Some people incorrectly interpret this historical fact to say that we have women prophets even today. However, not only are there no women foretelling God's future events—neither are there any men doing so. The reason for this is that all of God's intended information for us to be aware of...is already in the Bible.

In the Old Testament there were four *Major* Prophets and twelve *Minor* Prophets, and their Books bear their names in the last part of the Old Testament:

The four Major Prophets' Books appear in this order: Isaiah, Jeremiah who also wrote Lamentations, Ezekiel, and Daniel.

The twelve Minor Prophets were Hosea, Joel, Amos, Obadiah, Jonah, Micah, Nahum, Habakkuk, Zephaniah, Haggai, Zechariah, and Malachi. These twelve plus the four Major Prophets with Jeremiah's Book of Lamentations make up the last seventeen Books of the Old Testament.

There were *true* prophets and *false* prophets throughout the Scriptures, but the ones who were inspired by our God to prophesy future events, did so with many of their prophecies so far having later been fulfilled. For example, circa 580BC, Daniel prophesied the Temple that was to be rebuilt by 515BC would again be desolated. Then, approximately thirty-seven years before it happened, the Lord Jesus also prophesied that the Temple would be destroyed. Indeed it came to pass in the year AD 70. There are prophecies yet to be fulfilled which will begin with the Rapture and then continue into the end times.

Some claim that the most recent fulfillment was in 1948, less than seventy-five years ago. This was the year, on May 14, when the United States recognized Israel's national sovereignty, and, the next year, a United Nations resolution recognized Israel as, once again, a sovereign nation. They base this assertion upon the following verse:

> Who hath heard such a thing? Who hath seen such things? Shall the earth be made to bring forth [give birth] in one day? *Or* shall a nation be born at once? For as soon as Zion travailed [suffered in pains of labor], she brought forth her children. Isaiah 66:8

When one considers the Holocaust of the earlier 1940's and then Israel's sovereignty occurring only three years after the end of World War II, this Isaiah prophecy can certainly warrant a person to seek the truth. However, the verse does not specify the timing with precise dating, so discernment tells us that we should probably not be dogmatic about it.

In the Old Testament, the LORD God is quoted informing us of *false* prophets:

> Then the LORD said unto me, The prophets prophesy lies in my name: I sent them not, neither have I commanded them, neither spake unto them: they prophesy unto you a false vision and divination [Pagan fortune telling], and a thing of nought [worthless thing], and the deceit of their heart. Jeremiah 14:14

> IF there arise among you a prophet, or a dreamer of dreams, and giveth thee a sign or a wonder, [2]And the

sign or the wonder come to pass, whereof he spake unto thee, saying, Let us go after other gods, which thou has not known, and let us serve them, ³Thou shalt not hearken [listen] unto the words of that prophet, or that dreamer of dreams: for the LORD your God proveth [is testing] you, to know whether ye love the LORD your God with all your heart and with all your soul. Deuteronomy 13:1-3

When a prophet speaketh in the name of the LORD, if the thing follow not, nor come to pass, that *is* the thing which the LORD hath not spoken, *but* the prophet hath spoken it presumptuously: thou shalt not be afraid of him. Deuteronomy 18:22

True prophets in the Old and New Testaments not only foretold things to come, but also spoke the written Word of God, as do trustworthy brothers in Christ who bring forth the Word today.

It should be stressed once more: there are *no more future* prophecies to be prophesied. The completed Bible has all the prophecies that God has supernaturally instructed. We should exercise discernment and listen to His wisdom.

Therefore, all prophecies in the Bible have been fulfilled with the exception of the end times prophecies. Going into more detail; again these prophecies will be fulfilled when the end times predictions will begin upon Christ's return to the air to gather His Church believers in the air. This event is given a traditional name: the "Rapture". So, as of today, the end times are still in the future (unless the Rapture happens before the author has time to finish writing right now), but it could begin at any moment. In fact it could happen before reading the next sentence. If not, it could be before the sentence after that.

The Lord Jesus tells us that only His Father knows when the Father will send Him. This actually applies to both: the Rapture in the air and His Second Coming to earth. The two events will be separated by the seven-year *Tribulation.* His Second Coming to earth will put an end to that troublesome period of Almighty God's judgment. The believers of the Church Age will not be subjected to any of the wrath of God in this seven-year Tribulation, because the Rapture will occur prior to the Tribulation period. Therefore, the Rapture is the next prophecy to be fulfilled. God is pleading with us to heed His warnings. The Rapture will be followed by the Tribulation period. Matthew 24:36 refers to the *Second Coming* of Christ when He returns to this earth. Since we know He will return at the end of the last half of the seven-year Tribulation—a three and one-half year period called the *Great* Tribulation—it would seem reasonable to say that the Father's timing also applies to the Rapture since it will take place seven years prior to the end of the seven-year Tribulation period.

> But of that day and hour knoweth no *man*, no, not the angels of heaven, but my Father only. Matthew 24:36

> And he [Jesus] said unto them [His eleven apostles whom He had chosen (Acts 1:2)], It is not for you to know the times or the seasons, which the Father hath put in his own power [authority]. Acts 1:7

Even though John was a prisoner on the Island of Patmos, just off the Southwest coast of today's Turkey, his prophecies in the Book of Revelation are remarkably similar to what many of the prophets prophesied about the end times including the fall of Babylon and the war of Armageddon:

> [19]And Babylon, the glory of kingdoms, the beauty of the Chaldees' [Babylonians'] excellency, shall be as when

God overthrew Sodom and Gomorrah. [20]It shall never be inhabited, neither shall it be dwelt in from generation to generation... Isaiah 13:19-20a

Thus saith the LORD of hosts; The broad walls of Babylon shall be utterly broken [laid bare], and her high gates shall be burned with fire; and the people shall labor in vain, and the folk [*nations* because of the fire] in the fire, and they shall be weary. Jeremiah 51:58

We conclude that the events related to Babylon's capture in the sixth century B.C. and its eventual demise centuries later do not conform to the specific prophecies of Isaiah and Jeremiah [Rather they refer to the exile]. To date, for example, Babylon has never been destroyed by fire. Since the Lord says that it must be destroyed by fire, the rebuilding of a city known as "Babylon" is guaranteed (Rev. 18:10).[51]

Notable is God's wording of events in the Book of *The Revelation of Jesus Christ*—the last Book of the Bible, written circa AD 90-95, resembling those in the Old Testament. John the apostle describes how Babylon of the future will be destroyed:

[9]And the kings of the earth, who have committed fornication and lived deliciously [luxuriously] with her [Babylon], shall bewail [weep for] her, and lament for her, when they shall see the smoke of her burning, [10]Standing afar off for the fear of her torment, saying, Alas, alas, that great city Babylon, that mighty city! For in one hour is thy judgment come. Revelation 18:9-10

In what follows, the reader will notice a change in the order of chapter/verse reference at the end of the Scripture. The chapter/verse reference of the Old Testament will continue to come after the Scripture, but the New Testament chapter/verse reference will precede and be boldened to emphasize the fulfillment of the Old Testament Scripture:

> And I will plead [bring judgment to him] against him [the Antichrist man] with pestilence and with blood [bloodshed]; and I will rain upon him, and upon his bands [troops], and upon the many people [peoples] that *are* with him, and overflowing [flooding] rain, and great hailstones, fire, and brimstone. Ezekiel 38:22

> **Revelation 16:14, 21** [14]For they [the Antichrist man and the false prophet] are the spirits of devils [demons], working [performing signs], miracles, *which go* forth unto the kings of the earth and of the whole world, to gather them to the battle [Armageddon] of that great day of God Almighty.
> [21]And there fell upon men a great hail out of heaven, *every stone* about the weight of a talent [about eighty pounds]: and men blasphemed God because of the plague of the hail; for the plague thereof was exceeding great.

> [17]And, thou son of man, thus saith the Lord GOD; Speak unto every feathered fowl, and to every beast of the field, Assemble yourselves, and come; gather yourselves on every side to my sacrifice [sacrificial meal] that I do sacrifice for you, *even* a great sacrifice upon the mountains of Israel, that ye may eat flesh, and drink blood. [18]Ye shall eat the flesh of the mighty, and drink the blood of the princes of the earth, of rams, of lambs, and of goats, of bullocks [bulls], all of them fatlings of Bashan [Northern region of Palestine]. [19]And ye shall eat fat till ye be full, and drink blood till ye be drunken

[drunk], of my sacrifice [sacrificial meal] which I have sacrificed for you. [20]Thus ye shall be filled at my table with horses and chariots [riders], with mighty men, and with all men of war, saith the Lord GOD. [21]And I will set my glory among the heathen [nations], and all the heathen shall see my judgment that I have executed, and my hand that I have laid upon them. Ezekiel 39:17-21

Revelation 19:17-21 [17]And I saw an angel standing in the sun; and he cried with a loud voice, saying to all the fowls [birds] that fly in the midst of heaven, Come and gather yourselves together unto the supper of the great God; [18]That ye may eat the flesh of kings, and the flesh of captains, and the flesh of mighty men, and the flesh of horses, and of them that sit on them, and the flesh of all *men, both* free and bond [slave], both small and great. [19]And I saw the beast [the Antichrist man], and the kings of the earth, and their armies, gathered together to make war against him that sat on the horse [Christ Jesus on a white horse, Rev. 19:11], and against his army [His Church]. [20]And the beast [Antichrist] was taken [captured], and with him the false prophet that wrought miracles [worked signs] before him [in His presence] , with which he deceived them that had received the mark of the beast, and them that worshiped his image. These both were cast alive into a lake of fire burning with brimstone. [21]And the remnant [rest] were slain with the sword of him that sat upon the horse, which *sword* proceeded out of his mouth: and all the fowls [birds] were filled with their flesh.

[2]Son of man [The name by which God called Ezekiel], set thy face against Gog, the land of Magog [a barbarous northern region], the chief prince [prince of Rosh] of

Meshech and Tubal, and prophesy against him. [3]And say, Thus saith the lord GOD; Behold, I *am* against thee, O Gog [heathen nation, people], the chief prince of Meshech and Tubal: [4]And I will turn thee back [around], and put hooks into thy jaws, and I will bring thee forth, and all thine army, horses and horsemen, all of them clothed [splendidly clothed] with all sorts *of armor, even* a great company *with* bucklers [a large shield], all of them handling swords: Ezekiel 38:2-4

Revelation 20:7-10 [7]And when the thousand years are expired [completed], Satan shall be loosed [released] out of his prison, [8]And shall go out to deceive the nations which are in the four quarters of the earth, Gog and Magog, to gather them together to battle: the number of whom *is* as the sand of the sea. [9]And they went up on the breadth of the earth, and compassed [surrounded] the camp of the saints about, and the beloved city: and fire came down from God out of heaven, and devoured them. [10]And the devil that deceived them was cast into the lake of fire and brimstone, where the beast [Antichrist] and the false prophet *are*, and shall be tormented day and night for ever and ever.

Daniel's prophecies of the Babylonian, Medo-Persian, Greek, and Roman empires rising and falling which occurred in secular history beyond Daniel's lifetime are powerful examples of God's all-knowing future events. Daniel lived from about 605BC to 530BC and wrote his prophecies from captivity in Babylon—prophecies which became fulfilled all the way into the third century AD. And there are more of his prophecies to be fulfilled during the seven-year Tribulation to come. As

Daniel was instructed by God, his prophecies were detailed and accurate...even to the date of the Savior's death by crucifixion.

1. The Babylon fifty-year Empire fell to Medo-Persia as prophesied in 539BC.
2. The Medo-Persian two-hundred year Empire fell to the Greek Empire as prophesied in 334BC.
3. The Greek three-hundred year Empire fell to the Roman Empire as prophesied in 27BC.
4. The Roman four-hundred-fifty year Empire fell as prophesied in AD 428.
5. From the date Nehemiah and his team began rebuilding the Jerusalem wall until the date of Jesus' crucifixion was 483 years after Nehemiah's workers began rebuilding the wall (Daniel 9:24-26) and 434 years after the wall was completed; exactly as prophesied by Daniel (Daniel 9:25-26).

Daniel and the other true prophets' prophecies, all with detailed accuracy, bring our minds to realize God's omniscience is a supernatural, amazing, mind-boggling ability which is beyond all human comprehension. Daniel's prophecies were fulfilled in all those years after his death to well beyond five-hundred-fifty years...so far. Daniel also prophesied, in agreement with the prophecy of Paul the apostle, the appearing of the Antichrist which will happen after the Rapture and will begin the Tribulation period. Paul's prophecy is in 2 Thessalonians 2. Following is the comparison of the two prophecies, looking first at Daniel's:

> [35b]*Even* to the time of the end: because *it is* yet for a time appointed. [36]And the king [the Antichrist] shall do according to his will; and he shall exalt himself, and magnify himself above every god, and shall speak

marvelous [unusual] things against the God of gods, and shall prosper till the indignation be accomplished: for that that is determined shall be done. [37]Neither shall he regard the God [gods] of his fathers, nor the desire of women, nor regard any god: for he shall magnify himself above all. Daniel 11:35b-37

Paul prophesies very close to the same in the New Testament:

[3]Let no man deceive you by any means: for *that day* [the Rapture] *shall not come*, except there come a falling away [apostasy] first, and that man of sin [the Antichrist] be revealed, the son of perdition; [4]Who opposeth [opposes] and exalteth himself above all that is called God, or that is worshiped; so that he as God sitteth in the temple of God, showing himself that he is God. ... [6]And now ye know what withholdeth [is restraining] that he [the Antichrist] might be revealed in his own time [The Antichrist's *own time* is his seven-year career of bestowing deceptions and persecutions]. [7]For the mystery [hidden truth] of iniquity [lawlessness] doth already work: only he who now letteth [restrains will do] *will let*, until he [the Holy Spirit with the Church] be taken out of the way [Raptured].
2 Thessalonians 2:3-4, 6-7

It would be good to pause at this point and realize that all the prophets, in both the Old Testament and the New Testament, were giving these stern warnings in great hope that people would *listen*. God does not desire to lose any souls. The question needs to be asked, "Why would God have inspired all of these words of violence into His Word?" The answer: God has such fervent love for all of us—*everyone*—all of whom He created:

> For God so loved the world... John 3:16a

> *As* I live, saith the Lord GOD, I have no pleasure in the death of the wicked; but that the wicked turn from his way and live: turn ye, from his way [repent] and live: turn ye from your evil ways; for why will ye die...? Ezekiel 33:11

> And be not conformed to this world: but be ye transformed by the renewing of your mind...Romans 12:2a

The intensely brutal words of advice from God's true prophets are given to their readers so that the minds and hearts could be stirred to contemplate belief. Bear in mind that the prophecies of the Old Testament that had to do with the temporary destruction of Jerusalem and the exile of the Jews are actual historical facts. All this has really come to pass. God keeps His promises... Wise men listen to advice. (Proverbs 12:15b)

Isaiah is the first Major Prophet listed of all Israel's prophets in the Old Testament. He also prophesied in Isaiah chapters 13, 24, and 34 the forthcoming bitterness in both the seven-year Tribulation Period and the exile of the southern Jewish kingdom of Judah; and the tragedies that will take place at the end of these times of troubles. After the exile, and beginning with Isaiah 24:2-4, the following passages are just some examples of how Isaiah agrees with John's prophecies in the Book of Revelation:

> [2]And it shall be, as with the people, so with the priest; as with the servant, so with his master; as with the maid, so with her mistress; as with the buyer, so with the seller, as with the lender, so with the borrower; as

with the taker of usury [creditor], so with the giver of usury [debtor] to him. [3]The land shall be utterly emptied, and utterly spoiled [plundered]: for the LORD hath spoken this word. [4]The earth mourneth [mourns] *and* fadeth away, the haughty [proud] people of the earth do languish [weaken]. Isaiah 24:2-4

Revelation 18:14-19 [14]And the fruits that thy soul lusted after [longed for] are departed from thee [you], and all things which were dainty [are rich] and goodly [splendid] are departed from thee, and thou [you] shalt find them no more at all. [15]The merchants of these things, which were made rich by her [city of Babylon, the mother of harlots and abominations of the earth (Revelation 17:5)], shall stand afar off for the fear of her torment, weeping and wailing, [16]And saying, Alas, alas, that great city, that was clothed in fine linen, and purple, and scarlet, and decked [adorned] with gold, and precious stones, and pearls! [17]For in one hour so great riches is come to nought [nothing]. And every shipmaster, and all the company [who travel in ships] in ships, and sailors, and as many as trade by sea, stood afar off, [18]And cried when they saw the smoke of her burning, saying, What *city is* like unto this great city! [19]And they cast dust on their heads, and cried, weeping and wailing, saying, Alas, alas, that great city, wherein were made rich all that had ships in the sea by reason of her costliness [wealth]! For in one hour is she made desolate [a wasteland].

Here in Revelation the prophecy describes the great city becoming a desolate wasteland; where in Isaiah 24:3 we read "The land shall be utterly emptied, and utterly spoiled." This is

going to be just part of the end result of the war of Armageddon. This battle will take place in the twelve mile wide valley-
plain of Megiddo. It is located in central northern Israel and
the West Bank region. It runs from the Mediterranean shore
to the Jordan Valley. Napoleon called it the "cockpit" battleground: "The most natural battleground of the whole earth". It
is interesting to compare below, the doom of Babylon by the
Medes in Isaiah 13:1-19 with the similarities of total devastation of the end times in Revelation 16:13-16; 17:14:

> THE burden [oracle or prophecy against] of Babylon,
> which Isaiah the son of Amoz did see. [2]Lift ye up a
> banner upon the high mountain, exalt [raise your] voice
> unto them, shake [wave your] hand, that they may go
> into the gates of the nobles. [3]I have commanded my
> sanctioned [set apart or consecrated] ones, I have also
> called my mighty ones for mine anger, *even* them that
> rejoice in my highness [exaltation]. [4]The noise of a mul-
> titude in the mountains, like as of a great [many] people;
> a tumultuous noise of the kingdoms of nations gathered
> together: the LORD of hosts mustereth the host of the
> battle. [5]They [The Medes in Isaiah's time compares to
> the raptured believers in the end times] come from a far
> country, from the end of heaven, *even* the LORD, and
> the weapons of his indignation, to destroy the whole
> land. [6]Howl ye; for the day of the LORD *is* at hand; it
> shall come as a destruction from the Almighty. [7]There-
> fore shall all hands be faint [fall limp], and every man's
> heart shall melt: [8]And they shall be afraid: pangs [sharp
> pains] and sorrows shall take hold of them; they shall
> be in pain as a woman that travaileth [in childbirth]:
> they shall be amazed one at another; their faces *shall be*
> as flames. [9]Behold, the day of the LORD cometh, cruel
> both with wrath and fierce anger, to lay the land deso-
> late: and he shall destroy the sinners thereof out of it.

[10]For the stars of heaven and the constellations thereof shall not give their light: the sun shall be darkened in his going forth, and the moon shall not cause her light to shine. [11]And I will punish the world for *their* evil, and the wicked for their iniquity; and I will cause the arrogancy of the proud to cease, and will lay low the haughtiness [pride] of the terrible [or tyrants]. [12]I will make a man more precious [rare] than fine gold; even a man than the golden wedge of Ophir. [13]Therefore I will shake the heavens, and the earth shall remove out of her place, in the wrath of the LORD of hosts, and in the day of his fierce anger. [14]And it shall be as the chased roe [hunted gazelle], and as a sheep that no man taketh [gathers] up: they shall every man turn to his own people, and flee every one into his own land. [15]Every one that is found shall be thrust through; and every one that is joined [captured] *unto them* shall fall by the sword. [16]Their children also shall be dashed to pieces before their eyes; their houses shall be spoiled [plundered], and their wives ravished. [17]Behold, I will stir up the Medes against them, which shall not regard [esteem] silver; and *as for* gold, they shall not delight in it. [18]*Their* bows also shall dash the young men to pieces; and they shall have no pity on the fruit of the womb; their eye shall not spare children. [19]And Babylon, the glory of kingdoms, the beauty of the Chaldees' shall be as when God overthrew Sodom and Gomorrah. Isaiah 13:1-19

Revelation 16:13-16 [13]And I [John, he who is prophesying] saw three unclean spirits like frogs *come* out of the mouth of the dragon [Satan], and out of the mouth of the beast [the Antichrist man], and out of the mouth of the false prophet [These three are the false trinity

—Satan taking the place of the Father, the Antichrist taking the place of Christ, and the false prophet taking the place of the Holy Spirit]. [14]For they [the unclean spirits like frogs that are coming out of the false trinity] are the spirits of devils [demons], working [performing signs] miracles, *which* go forth unto the kings of the earth and of the whole world, to gather them to the battle of that great day of God Almighty. [Next, the Lord Jesus is quoted:] [15]Behold, I come as a thief. Blessed *is* he that watcheth, and keepeth his garments, lest he walk naked; and they see his shame. [16]And he [the false trinity] gathered them together into a place called in the Hebrew tongue Armageddon [Lit. *Mount Megiddo* near the Kishon River and off the Valley of Jezreel; about twenty to twenty-five miles (about forty km) east of the Mediterranean Coast in NW Israel].

Revelation 17:14 These shall make war with the Lamb [Christ the Savior], and the Lamb shall overcome them: for he is Lord of lords, and King of kings: and they [the raptured believers] that are with him *are* called, and chosen, and faithful.

COME near, ye nations, to hear; and hearken, ye people: let the earth hear, and all that is therein; the world, and all things that come forth of it. [2]For the indignation of the LORD *is* upon all nations, and *his* fury upon all their armies: he hath utterly destroyed them, he hath delivered them to the slaughter. [3]Their slain also shall be cast out, and their stink shall come up out of their carcasses, and the mountains shall be melted with their blood. [4]And all the host of heaven shall be dissolved, and the heavens shall be rolled together as a scroll: and all their host shall fall down, as the leaf falleth off from

the vine, and as a falling *fig* from the fig tree.
Isaiah 34:1-4

[7]But the heavens and the earth, which are now, by the same word are kept in store, reserved unto fire against [until] the day of judgment and perdition [destruction] of ungodly men. ...
[10]But the day of the Lord will come as a thief [robber] in the night; in which the heavens shall pass away with a great noise, and the elements shall melt with fervent heat, the earth also and the works that are therein shall be burned up. 2 Peter 3:7, 10

Revelation 6:12-17 [12]And I beheld when he [the Lord Jesus] had opened the sixth seal, and, lo, there was a great earthquake; and the sun became black as sackcloth of hair, and the moon became as blood; [13]And the stars of heaven fell unto the earth, even as a fig tree casteth her untimely figs [drops its late figs], when she is shaken of a mighty wind. [14]And the heaven departed [sky split apart] as a scroll when it is rolled together; and every mountain and island were moved out of their places. [15]And the kings of the earth, and the great men, and the rich men, and the chief captains, and the mighty men, and every bondman [slave], and every free man, hid themselves in the dens [caves] and in the rocks of the mountains; [16]And said to the mountains and rocks, Fall on us, and hide us from the face of him [Father God] that sitteth on the throne, and from the wrath of the Lamb. [17]For the great day of his wrath is come; and who shall be able [is able] to stand?

Concerning the *untimely fig tree* analogy, the Major Prophet Jeremiah writes what the LORD speaks:

⁸And as the evil [bad] figs, which cannot be eaten, they are so evil; surely thus saith the LORD, So will I give Zedekiah the king of Judah, and his princes, and the residue of Jerusalem, that remain in this land, and them that dwell in the land of Egypt: ⁹And I will deliver them to be removed into all the kingdoms of the earth [to trouble; tribulation] for *their* hurt [harm], *to be* a reproach and a proverb [byword], a taunt and a curse, in all places whither [wherever] I shall drive them. ¹⁰And I will send the sword, the famine, and the pestilence, among them, till they be consumed [destroyed] from off the land that I gave unto them and to their fathers. Jeremiah 24:8-10

Jeremiah is known by many as *the prophet of the broken heart*. He had love much like that of God for all people. He implored the sinners to repent of their ways and turn to God so that God would turn His wrath from them:

¹¹And this whole land shall be a desolation, *and* an astonishment; and these nations shall serve the king of Babylon seventy years. ¹²And it shall come to pass, when seventy years are accomplished, *that* I will punish the king of Babylon, and that nation, saith the LORD, for their iniquity [sin], and the land of the Chaldeans [Babylonians], and will make it perpetual desolations. Jeremiah 25:11-12

¹⁵For thus saith the LORD God of Israel unto me; Take the wine cup of this fury [wrath] at my hand, and cause all the nations, to whom I send thee, to drink it. ... ²⁶And all the kings of the north, far and near, one with another, and all the kingdoms of the world, which *are* upon the face of the earth: and the king of Sheshach

[code word for Babylon] shall drink after them. [27]Therefore thou shalt say unto them, Thus saith the LORD of hosts, the God of Israel; Drink ye, and be drunken [drunk], and spew [vomit], and fall, and rise no more, because of the sword which I will send among you. [28]And it shall be, if they refuse to take the cup at thine hand to drink, then shalt thou say unto them, Thus saith the LORD of hosts; Ye shall certainly drink. [The cup is a symbol of divine judgment.] [29]For, lo, I [cause you to] begin to bring evil [calamity] on the city which is called by my name [Jerusalem means *the habitation of peace*, and it is God's chosen city for His divine Kingship.], and should ye be utterly unpunished? Ye shall not be unpunished: for I will call for a sword upon all the inhabitants of the earth, saith the LORD of hosts. Jeremiah 25:15, 26-29

If so be they will hearken [listen], and turn every man from his evil way, that I may repent me of the evil [relent of the calamity], which I purpose to do unto them because of the evil of their doings. Jeremiah 26:3

[2]Declare ye among the nations, and publish [proclaim], and set up a standard [lift up a banner]; publish, *and* conceal not: say, Babylon is taken, Bel [a Babylonian god] is confounded, Merocach [a Babylonian god] is broken in pieces; her idols are confounded [humiliated], her images are broken in pieces... [9]For, lo, I will raise and cause to come up against Babylon an assembly of great nations from the north country: and they shall set themselves in array against her; from thence she shall be taken [captured]: their arrows *shall be* as of a mighty expert man [an expert warrior]; none shall return in vain. [10]And Chaldea shall be a spoil

[become plunder]: all that spoil [plunder] her shall be satisfied, saith the LORD...

¹²Your mother shall be sore confounded [deeply ashamed]; she that bare you shall be ashamed: behold, the hindermost [least] of the nations *shall* be a wilderness, a dry land, and a desert. ¹³Because of the wrath of the LORD it shall not be inhabited, but it shall be wholly desolate: every one that goeth by Babylon shall be astonished [horrified], and hiss at all her plagues...

¹⁵Shout against her round about: she hath given her hand: her foundations are fallen, her walls are thrown down: for it *is* the vengeance of the LORD: take vengeance upon her; as she hath done, do unto her...

²²A sound of battle *is* in the land, and of great destruction. ²³How is the hammer of the whole earth cut asunder [apart] and broken! How is Babylon become a desolation among the nations! ...

²⁵The LORD hath opened his armory, and hath brought forth the weapons of his indignation: for this *is* the work of the Lord GOD of hosts in the land of the Chaldeans. Jeremiah 50:2, 9-10, 12-13, 15, 22-23, 25

Revelation 16:17-21 ¹⁷And the seventh angel poured out his vial [bowl] into the air; and there came a great voice out of the temple of heaven, from the throne, saying, It is done. ¹⁸And there were voices, and thunders, and lightnings; and there was a great earthquake, such as was not since men were upon the earth, so mighty an earthquake, *and* so great. ¹⁹And the great city was divided into three parts, and the cities of the nations fell: and great Babylon came in remembrance before God, to give unto her the cup of the wine of the fierceness of his wrath. ²⁰And every island fled away, and the mountains were not found. ²¹And there fell upon men a great hail out of heaven, *every stone* about the weight of a talent [about eighty pound hail balls]: and men blasphemed God because of the plague of the hail; for the plague thereof was exceeding great.

Again, in order to understand a prophet's writings, the reader sometimes needs to understand that the writer was envisioning the future, but was writing with past tense. The reason for this is that he was writing about what he *had seen* in a vision or what he *had heard* from God.

Some of the Twelve Minor Prophets

All of the four Old Testament Major Prophets included prophecies that are in agreement with the prophecies of John in the Book of *The Revelation of Jesus Christ*. Some of the Minor Prophets are included as well:

The earth shall quake before them; the heavens shall tremble: the sun and the moon shall be dark, and the stars shall withdraw [diminish their brightness] their shining. Joel 2:10

The sun shall be turned into darkness, and the moon into blood, before the great and the terrible day of the LORD come. Joel 2:31

[15]The sun and moon shall be darkened, and the stars shall withdraw their shining. [16a]The LORD also shall roar out of Zion [just SE of Jerusalem Old City wall], and utter his voice from Jerusalem; and the heavens and the earth shall shake: but the LORD *will* be the hope of his people, Joel 3:15-16a

While the Lord Jesus Himself was later also fully Man, He said the same thing:

> Immediately after the tribulation of those days shall the sun be darkened, and the moon shall not give her light, and the stars shall fall from heaven, and the powers of the heavens shall be shaken. Matthew 24:29

The prophet Zephaniah prophecies more of the same:

> [14]The great day of the LORD *is* near, *it is* near, and hasteth [hurries] greatly, *even* the voice [noise] of the day of the LORD: the mighty man shall cry there bitterly. [15]That day *is* a day of wrath, a day of trouble and distress, a day of wasteness [devastation] and desolation, a day of darkness and gloominess, a day of clouds and thick darkness, [16]A day of the trumpet and alarm against the fenced [fortified] cities, and against the high towers. [17]And I will bring distress upon men, that they shall walk like blind men, because they have sinned against the LORD: and their blood shall be poured out as dust, and their flesh as the dung [refuse for sewage]. [18]Neither their silver nor their gold shall be able to deliver them in the day of the LORD'S wrath; but the whole land shall be devoured by the fire of his jealousy: for he shall make even a speedy riddance [end] of all them that dwell in the land. Zephaniah 1:14-18

Joel also prophesied in agreement with the sounding of the fifth trumpet in Revelation:

> BLOW ye the trumpet [ram's horn] in Zion, and sound an alarm in my holy mountain: let all the inhabitants of the land tremble: for the day of the LORD cometh, for *it is* nigh at hand: [2]A day of darkness and of gloominess,

a day of clouds and of thick darkness, as the morning spread upon the mountains: a great people and a strong [mighty, powerful people]; there hath not been ever the like, neither shall be any more after it, *even* to the years of many generations. [3]A fire devoureth before them; and behind them a flame burneth: the land *is* as the garden of Eden before them, and behind them a desolate wilderness; yea, and nothing shall escape them. [4]The appearance of them *is* as the appearance of horses; and as horsemen [swift steeds], so shall they run. [5]Like the noise of chariots on the tops of mountains shall they leap, like the noise of a flame of fire that devoureth the stubble, as a strong people set in battle array. [6]Before their face the people shall be much pained: all faces shall [be drained of color] gather blackness. [7]They shall run like mighty men; they shall climb the wall like men of war; and they shall march every one on his ways [in formation], and they shall not break their ranks:
Joel 2:1-7

The Old Testament prophet Nahum also includes likenesses to the Book of Revelation. Nahum's description of the warnings and *temporary* ruin of Nineveh resembles the *permanent* devastation of the city of Babylon—an eternal destruction figurative of man's wickedness and God's judgment:

WOE to the bloody city! [2]The noise of a whip, and the noise of the rattling of the wheels, and of the prancing [galloping] horses, and of the jumping [jolting] chariots. [3]The horsemen lifteth up [charge with] both the bright sword and the glittering spear: and *there is* a multitude of slain, and a great number of carcasses; and *there is* none end [are countless] of *their* corpses: [4]Because of the multitude of the whoredoms [harlotries, spiritual unfaithfulness] of the well-favored [seductive] harlot, the mistress of witchcrafts [sorceries], that selleth nations through her whoredoms, and families through her witchcrafts. [5]Behold, I *am* against thee, saith the LORD of hosts; and I will discover [lift] thy skirts upon [over] thy face, and I will show the nations thy nakedness, and the kingdoms thy shame. [6]And I will cast abominable filth upon thee, and make thee vile [impure, sinful in the sight of God and good men], and will set thee as a gazingstock [spectacle]. [7]And it shall come to pass, *that* all they that look upon thee shall flee from thee, and say, Nineveh is laid waste: who will bemoan [express sorrow for] her? whence shall I seek comforters for thee? [On July 24, 2014 radical Islamic terrorists (ISIS) destroyed the memorial of Jonah in Mosul (Nineveh), Iraq.[52]] [8]Art thou better than populous No [*No* was populous Alexandria; Amon, ancient Thebes on the Nile River], that was situate [situated] among the rivers, *that had* the waters round about it, whose rampart *was* the sea, *and* her wall *was* from the sea? [9]Ethiopia and Egypt *were* her strength, and *it was* infinite [boundless]; Put and Lubim [descendant of Ham and the Persian tribe *Lubim*] were thy [her] helpers. [10]Yet *was* she carried away, she went into captivity: her young children also were dashed in pieces at the top [head] of all the streets: and they cast lots for her honorable men, and all her great men were bound in chains. [11]Thou also shalt be drunken [drunk]: thou shalt be hid, thou also shalt seek strength because of [refuge from] the enemy. [12]All thy strongholds *shall be like* fig trees with the firstripe figs: if they be shaken, they shall even fall into the mouth of the eater. [13]Behold, thy people in the midst of thee *are* women: the gates of thy land shall be set wide open unto thine enemies: the fire shall devour thy [gate bars] bars. [14]Draw thee waters for the siege, fortify thy strongholds: go into clay, and tread the mortar, make strong the brickkiln [a pile of brick constructed for heating and hardening clay mortar]. [15]There shall the fire devour thee; the sword shall cut thee off, it shall eat thee up like the cankerworm [locust]: make thyself many as the cankerworm, make thyself many as the locusts [swarming locusts]. [16]Thou hast multiplied thy merchants above the stars of heaven: the cankerworm spoileth [locust plunders], and flieth away. [17]Thy crowned [commanders, officials] *are* as the locusts [swarming locusts], and thy captains as the great grasshoppers, which camp in the hedges in the cold day, *but* when the sun ariseth they flee away, and their place is not known where they *are*. [18]Thy shepherds slumber, O king of Assyria: thy nobles shall dwell [rest] *in the dust*: thy people is scattered upon the mountains, and no man gathereth *them*. [19]*There is* no healing of thy bruise [injury]; thy wound is grievous [severe]: all that hear the bruit [news] of thee shall clap the hands over thee: for upon whom hath not thy wickedness passed continually? Nahum 3:1-19

Revelation 9:7-12 [7]And the shapes of the locusts *were* like unto horses prepared unto battle; and on their heads *were* as it were crowns like gold, and their faces *were* as the faces of men. [8]And they had hair as the hair of women, and their teeth were as *the teeth* of lions. [9]And they had breastplates, as it were breastplates of iron; and the sound of their wings *was* as the sound of chariots of many horses running to battle. [10]And they had tails like unto scorpions, and there were stings in their tails: and their power [authority] *was* to hurt men five months. [11]And they had a king over them, *which is* the angel of the bottomless pit, whose name in the

Hebrew tongue *is* Abaddon [Destruction], but in the Greek tongue hath *his* name Apollyon [*Destroyer*—Satan who gives demonic supernatural authority to the Antichrist and false prophet]. [12]One woe is past; *and,* behold, there come two woes more hereafter.

The Minor Prophet Zechariah is also in agreement with the foretelling of things of the Day of the Lord:

[2]And said unto me, What seest thou? And I said, I have looked, and behold a candlestick [lampstand] all *of* gold, with a bowl upon the top of it, and his seven lamps thereon, and seven pipes to the seven lamps, which *are* upon the top thereof: [3]And two olive trees by *it* [a seven lamp candlestick], one upon the right *side* of the bowl, and the other upon the left *side* thereof. ...

[11]Then answered I, and said unto him, What *are* these two olive trees upon the right *side* of the candlestick [lampstand] and upon the left *side* thereof? ...

[14]Then said he, These *are* the two anointed ones [sons of fresh oil], that stand by the Lord of the whole earth. [Although, in Zechariah's time the context is referring to Joshua, the high priest, and Zerubbabel, the governor, this passage also lines up with the two anointed witnesses of Revelation chapter 11.]

Zechariah 4:2-3, 11, 14

Revelation 11:3-6 [3]And I will give *power* unto my two witnesses, and they shall prophesy a thousand two hundred *and* threescore [sixty] days, clothed in sackcloth. [4]These are the two olive trees, and the two candlesticks [lampstands] standing before the God of the earth. [5]And if any man will hurt them, fire proceedeth out of their mouth, and devoureth their enemies: and if any man will hurt them, he must in this manner be killed. [6]These have power [authority] to shut heaven, that it rain not in the days of their prophecy: and have power over waters to turn them to blood, and to smite the earth with all plagues, as often as they will.

Zechariah is compared to Revelation in Satan's presence to resist and accuse believers:

AND he showed me Joshua the high priest standing before the angel of the LORD, and Satan standing at his right had to resist him. Zechariah 3:1

Revelation 12:10 And I heard a loud voice saying in heaven, Now is come salvation, and strength, and the kingdom of our God [referring to the coming Millennial Kingdom of Christ], and the power of his Christ: for the accuser [Satan] of our brethren is cast down, which accused them before our God day and night.

Revelation 14:8 And there followed another angel, saying, Babylon is fallen, is fallen, that great city, because she made all nations drink of the wine of the wrath of her fornication.

The Major Prophet Jeremiah warns of the devastation to come (from the Medes in Jeremiah's time):

[6]Flee out of the midst of Babylon, and deliver every man his soul [life]: be not cut off in her iniquity; for this *is* the time of the LORD'S vengeance; he will render unto her a recompense. [7]Babylon *hath been* a golden cup in the LORD'S hand, that made all the earth drunken: the nations drunken of her wine; therefore the nations

are mad [deranged]. [8a]Babylon is suddenly fallen and destroyed: howl [wail] for her, Jeremiah 51:6-8a

[13]Put ye in the sickle [a reaping, gathering, pruning hooked tool], for the harvest is ripe [for judgment of the wicked]: come, get you down; for the press [winepress] is full, the vats overflow; for their wickedness *is* great. [14]Multitudes, multitudes in the valley of decision: for the day of the LORD *is* near in the valley of decision. Joel 3:13-14

Revelation 14:14-20 [14]And I looked, and behold a white cloud, and upon the cloud *one* sat like unto the Son of man, having on his head a golden crown, and in his hand a sharp sickle. [15]And another angel came out of the temple, crying with a loud voice to him that sat on the cloud, Thrust in thy sickle, and reap: for the time is come for thee to reap; for the harvest of the earth is ripe [for judgment]. [16]And he that sat on the cloud thrust in his sickle on the earth; and the earth was reaped. [17]And another angel came out of the temple which is in heaven, he also having a sharp sickle. [18]And another angel came out from the altar, which had power over fire; and cried with a loud cry to him that had the sharp sickle, saying, Thrust thy sharp sickle, and gather the clusters of the vine of the earth; for her grapes [heathen] are fully ripe [for judgment]. [19]And the angel thrust in his sickle into the earth, and gathered the vine of the earth, and cast *it* into the great wine press of the wrath of God. [20]And the winepress was trodden [trampled] without [outside] the city, and blood came out of the winepress, even unto the horse bridles, by the space of a thousand *and* six hundred furlongs [Gr. *Stadia*, about one hundred-eighty-four miles].

And *men* shall dwell in it, and there shall be no more utter destruction; but Jerusalem shall be safely inhabited. Zechariah 14:11

Revelation 22:3 And there shall be no more curse: but the throne of God and of the Lamb *shall* be in it; and his servants shall serve him.

Those who heard but did not heed the admonitions from the Old Testament prophets suffered exile, and many, even died premature deaths. Those prophecies did, in fact, come to pass. Today, the vast majority (Matthew 7:13-14) who prefer to ignore John's prophetic message in the Book of Revelation, are bound for eternal suffering. Sadly, after all those warnings from both the Old and the New Testament prophets, people, even today, still opt not to admit guilt and to repent of their sins, and they choose not to believe God's very Word. John prophesied that the Israelites' conduct will actually be repeated:

Revelation 9:21 Neither repented they of their murders, nor of their sorceries, nor of their fornication, nor of their thefts.

Now that we have seen a multitude of harsh warnings, let us exalt the Lord Jesus Christ who saves all who repent and believe what John has also prophesied. Today's believers need not worry about all those prophecies of the Tribulation period that will, indeed, *soon* be fulfilled, because the Lord Jesus gave His life and blood to save those who sincerely repent and believe:

Much more then, being justified [to not be seen by God as being wicked, but to be righteous in God's view] by his blood, we shall be saved from wrath through him. Romans 5:9

"Jesus had peasant parents, was in a manger-bed, and He was humble with fishermen as His choice for disciples."[53]

We rely on the *truth* of the scriptural prophecies.[54]

Isaiah 53:1-12 Prophecies of Christ's Death and Resurrection Fulfilled

Jesus humbled himself and obeyed the Father to the point of death on the cross (Philippians 2:8). In the Old Testament, Isaiah Chapters 52 and 53 give a perfect example of this when, circa 700BC, prophesying the suffering of Christ Jesus, in twelve verses, fifteen Messianic (the Christ—Savior) prophecies are fulfilled. All but two of the fifteen verses in Isaiah 53 contain *fulfillment* of Isaiah's prophecies in the New Testament Gospels of Matthew, Mark, Luke, and John; as well as in other New Testament Books:

Messiah is the Hebrew translation of *Christ*—the Lord God our Savior. Samples of these Messianic prophecies and their fulfillments in the Isaiah passage 53:1-12 are provided below. The following list does not include the three previous verses to chapter 53: Isaiah 52:13-15—which are also Messianic prophecies that Christ has fulfilled. Take note that the title of this section points out that all of these prophesies were fulfilled nearly 2,000 years ago, and all accomplished for the believer's benefit of everlasting life.

Isaiah 53:1: WHO hath believed our report? And to whom is the arm [the power] of the LORD revealed?

Isaiah 53:1 prophecy fulfilled in the New Testament:

> [37]But though he had done so many miracles [signs] before them, yet they believed not on him: [38]That the saying of Isaiah the prophet might be fulfilled, which he spake, LORD, WHO HATH BELIEVED OUR REPORT? AND TO WHOM HATH THE ARM OF THE LORD BEEN REVEALED? John 12:37-38

> **Isaiah 53:3a**: "He is despised and rejected [forsaken] of men;"

Isaiah 53:3a prophecy fulfilled in the New Testament:

> He [Jesus] came unto his own, and his own received him not. John 1:11

> But I [David's prophesied view of Christ on the cross] *am* a worm, and no man; a reproach of men, and despised of the people. Psalm 22:6

> **Isaiah 53b**: a man of sorrows [pains], and acquainted with grief [sickness], He healed many: and we hid as it were *our* faces from him; he was despised, and we esteemed him not.

Isaiah 53:3b prophecy fulfilled in the New Testament:

> [16]When the even [evening] was come, they brought unto him many that were possessed with devils [demons]: and he cast out the spirits with *his* word, and healed all that were sick: [17]That it might be fulfilled which was spoken by Isaiah the prophet, saying, HIMSELF TOOK OUR INFIRMITIES, AND BARE *OUR* INFIRMITIES, AND BARE OUR SICKNESSES. Matthew 8:16-17

Isaiah 53:4: Surely he hath borne our griefs [sicknesses], and carried our sorrows [pains]: yet we did esteem [reckon] him stricken, smitten of [struck down by] God, and afflicted.

Isaiah 53:4 prophecy fulfilled in the New Testament:

[30]And they spit upon him, and took the reed, and smote [struck] him on the head. [31]And after that they had mocked him, they took the robe off from him, and put his own raiment [clothes] on him, and led him away to crucify *him...*

[35a]And they crucified him...

[39]And they that passed by reviled [blasphemed] him, wagging their heads, Matthew 27:30-31, 35a, 39

THEN Pilate therefore took Jesus, and scourged [*whipped Him with a Roman scourge*: a whip designed for inflicting torturous pain with severe wounds] *him.* [2]And the soldiers plaited [twisted] a crown of thorns, and put *it* on his head, and they put on him a purple robe [a way of mocking Him since kings wore crowns and purple robes], And said, Hail, King of the Jews! and they smote him with their hands. John 19:1-3

[67]Then did they spit in his face, and buffeted [beat] him; and others smote [struck] *him* with the palms of their hands [or rods], [68]Saying, Prophesy unto us, thou Christ, Who is he that smote [struck] thee? Matthew 26:67-68

[63]And the men that held Jesus mocked him, and smote [beat] *him.* [64]And when they had blindfolded him, they struck him on the face, and asked him, saying, Prophesy, who is it that smote [struck] thee? Luke 22:63-64

[31]Then he [Jesus] took *unto him* the twelve, and said unto them, Behold, we go up to Jerusalem, and all things that are written by the prophets concerning the Son of man shall be accomplished [fulfilled]. [32]For he shall be delivered unto the Gentiles, and shall be mocked, and spitefully [insulted] entreated, and spitted on: [33]And they shall scourge *him*, and put him to death: and the third day he shall rise again. Luke 18:31-33

Isaiah 53:5: But he *was* wounded for our transgressions, *he was* bruised for our iniquities: the chastisement of our peace *was* upon him; and with his stripes we are healed.

Isaiah 53:5 prophecy and Daniel 9:24, 26 prophecies fulfilled in the New Testament:

[6]For when we were yet without strength, in due time [at the *right time*; even the exact time Daniel prophesied it would occur (Dan. 9:26)] Christ died for the ungodly...
[8]But God commendeth [demonstrates] his love toward us, in that, while we were yet sinners, Christ died for us. Romans 5:6, 8

Seventy weeks [Lit. seventy *sevens*, Hebrew translation gives 490 years (seven years of which will come during the Tribulation period and end at the Second Coming and soon beginning of Christ's Millennial reign; so 483 years from when the Temple was rebuilt (Ezra 6:15) until Christ's crucifixion] are determined upon thy people and upon thy holy city, to finish the transgression, and to make an end of sins [during the peaceful Millennial reign], and to make reconciliation for iniquity, and to bring an everlasting righteousness, and to seal up the vision and prophecy, and anoint the most Holy [Holy of Holies]. Daniel 9:24

In other words, Daniel prophesied 483 years from rebuilding the temple until the Christ would be crucified, but there would then be a pause—the Church Age—*and then* the Rapture immediately followed by the seven-year Tribulation. Those seven years added to the 483 years accounts for the total *seventy sevens* which equates to 490 years.

> And after threescore and two weeks [Hebrew translation gives 434 years from when Jerusalem wall was rebuilt until Christ was crucified.] shall Messiah be cut off... Daniel 9:26a

The end of the 483 years in Daniel 9:24 and the end of the 434 years in Daniel 9:26 both fall on the exact date of the Savior's crucifixion. If need be, the following is a more detailed explanation: For the "threescore and two weeks" to be thoroughly understood, in Hebrew a *week* can mean seven years—and in the context here, a week does translate to seven years. Warren Henderson explains it well:

> Both the starting point [the time Nehemiah's workers began rebuilding the wall] and the ending point [Christ's crucifixion] of Daniel's prophecy are fixed. [The prophecy declared there would be sixty-nine weeks—or sixty-nine back-to-back seven-year periods from beginning to end. (69 x 7 = 483 years)] A Jewish year is 360 days; 360 x 483 = 173,880 days. These 173,880 days are the number of days from the command of Artaxerxes Longimanus to Nehemiah to rebuild the wall about Jerusalem (March 14, 445 B.C.) until Messiah's final presentation in Jerusalem (April 6, AD 32) and subsequent death. The

exact date will vary depending on the chronology used to date the command to rebuild. But like Jeremiah's seventy-week [seventy-year fulfilled] prophecies [from Jewish exile to being sent back, Jer. 25:12; 29:10], the sixty-nine-week portion of Daniel's prophecy has been fulfilled. The final week, associated with the Jewish nation, will begin with the signing of a covenant with the Antichrist.[55]

Only God could give a prophet the vision of such precise foretelling as this. God's incredible Word is absolute truth.

> Isaiah 53:6: All we like sheep have gone astray; we have turned every one to his own way; and the LORD hath laid on him the iniquity of us all.

Isaiah 53:6 prophecy fulfilled in the New Testament:
For all have sinned, and come short of the glory of God. Romans 3:23

> [24]But for us also, to whom it [salvation] shall be imputed [accredited], if we believe on him that raised up Jesus our Lord from the dead; [25]Who was delivered for our offenses, and was raised again for our justification [justified to have the righteousness of God—which He gives to us when we believe—and, which is required by Him for us to be with Him]. Romans 4:24-25

> [5]Even when we were dead in sins, [God] hath quickened [made us alive] us together with Christ, (by grace ye are [have been] saved;) [6]And hath raised *us* up together, and made *us* sit together in heavenly *places* in Christ Jesus: [7]That in the ages to come he might show the exceeding

riches of his grace in *his* kindness toward us through Christ Jesus. [8]For by grace are ye [you have been] saved through faith; and that not of yourselves: *it is* the gift of God: [9]Not of works, lest any man should boast. Ephesians 2:5-9

[3]For we ourselves were sometimes foolish, disobedient, deceived, serving divers lusts and pleasures, living in malice and envy, hateful, *and* hating one another. [4]But after that the kindness and love of God our Savior toward man appeared, [5]Not by works of righteousness which we have done, but according to his mercy he saved us, by the washing of regeneration, and renewing of the Holy Ghost; [6]Which he shed [poured out] on us abundantly through Jesus Christ our Savior Titus 3:3-6

Isaiah 53:7: He was oppressed, and he was afflicted, yet he opened not his mouth: he is [was led] brought as a lamb to the slaughter, and as a sheep before her shearers is dumb, so he openeth not his mouth.

Isaiah 53:7 prophecy fulfilled in the New Testament:
[12]And when he [Jesus] was accused of the chief Priests and elders, he answered nothing. [13]Then said Pilate unto him, Hearest thou not how many things they witness [testify] against thee? [14]And he answered him to never a word; insomuch that the governor marveled greatly. Matthew 27:12-14

[3]And the chief priests accused him of many things: but he answered nothing. [4]And Pilate asked him again, saying, Answereth thou nothing? Behold how many things they witness [testify] against thee. [5]But Jesus answered nothing; so that Pilate marveled. Mark 15:3-5

⁵Then came Jesus forth, wearing the crown of thorns, and the purple robe. And *Pilate* saith unto them, Behold the man! ⁶When the chief priests therefore and officers saw him, they cried out saying, Crucify *him,* crucify *him.* Pilate saith unto them, Take ye him [you all take Him], and crucify *him*: for I find no fault in him. ⁷The Jews answered him, We have a law, and by our law he ought to die, because he made himself the Son of God. ⁸When Pilate therefore heard that saying, he was the more afraid; ⁹And went again into the judgment hall, and saith unto Jesus, Whence art thou [Where are You from]? But Jesus gave him no answer. John 19:5-9

The Old Testament *law* the Jews were referring to was that if anyone claimed to be God who wasn't truly God, the false claim was called *blasphemy*:

And he that blasphemeth the name [wrongly take the Name] of the LORD, he shall surely be put to death, Leviticus 24:16a

But, indeed, the Lord Jesus Christ is truly One of the Three Persons of God:

⁶Who, being in the form of God, thought it not robbery to be equal with God: ⁷But made himself of no reputation, and took upon him the form of a servant, and was made [was coming] in the likeness of men: ⁸And being found in fashion [appearance] as a man, he humbled himself, and became obedient unto death, even the death of the cross. Philippians 2:6-8

Isaiah 53:8: He was taken from prison [out of oppression] and from judgment [from justice to injustice]: and who shall declare [consider His potential life *among His generation* had He not been crucified] his generation? For he was cut off out of the land of the living: for the transgression of my people he was stricken.

Isaiah 53:8 prophecy fulfilled in the New Testament:
[28]Then led they Jesus from Caiaphas unto the hall [Gr. *Praetorian,* the governor's headquarters] of judgment: and it was early; and they themselves went not into the judgment hall, lest they should be defiled; but that they might eat the passover. [29]Pilate then went out unto them, and said, What accusation bring ye against this man? [30]They answered and said unto him, If he were not a malefactor [evildoer], we would not have delivered him up unto thee. John 18:28-30

WHEN the morning was come, all the chief priests and elders of the people took counsel against Jesus to put him to death: [2]And when they had bound him, they led *him* away, and delivered him to Pontius Pilate the governor [the Roman governor of Judea and Samaria]. Matthew 27:1-2

The last sentence in Isaiah 53:8 prophesied that Jesus Christ [Messiah] would be "cut off out of the land of the living." Daniel prophesied the same thing two hundred years after Isaiah prophesied it—and nearly five hundred years before Christ was put to death on the cross.

And after threescore and two weeks shall Messiah be cut off ["cut off out of the land of the living" (Isaiah 53:8) by suffering the death penalty] Daniel 9:26a

The agreement with Isaiah and Christ's fulfillment are mind boggling and the accuracy of Daniel's prophecy is amazing—to the very day of foretelling when Christ would be crucified!

> **Isaiah 53:9**: And he made his grave with the wicked, and with the rich in his death; because he had done no violence, neither *was any* deceit in his mouth.

Isaiah 53:9 prophecy fulfilled in the New Testament:

> [57]When the even [evening] was come, there came a rich man of Arimathea, named Joseph, who also himself was Jesus' disciple [student, follower]: [58]He went to Pilate, and begged [asked for] the body of Jesus. Then Pilate commanded the body to be delivered. [59]And when Joseph had taken the body, he wrapped it in a clean linen cloth, [60]And laid it in his own new tomb, which he had hewn out in the rock: and he rolled a great stone to the door of the sepulcher [tomb], and departed. Matthew 27:57-60

> [42]And now when the even [evening] was come, because it was the preparation, that is, the day before the sabbath, [43]Joseph of Arimathea, an honorable counselor [prominent council member], which also waited for the kingdom of God [means he believed], came, and went in boldly unto Pilate, and craved [asked for] the body of Jesus. [44]And Pilate marveled if he were already dead: and calling *unto him* the centurion, he asked him whether he had been any while [a long time] dead. [45]And when he knew *it* [learned] of the centurion, he gave the body to Joseph. [46]And he [Joseph] bought fine linen, and took him down [from the cross], and wrapped him in linen, and laid him in a sepulcher [tomb] which was hewn out

of a rock, and rolled a stone unto the door of the sepulcher. [47]And Mary Magdalene and Mary *the mother* of Joses beheld where he was laid. Mark 15:42-47

Some may question Mary being the mother of Jōsēs. It can be confusing since one of the brothers of Jesus was named Jōsēs. However, one of the twelve disciples, James the Less, also had a brother named Jōsēs, and their mother was named Mary:

> There were also women looking on afar off: among whom was Mary Magdalene, and Mary the mother of James the less and of Joses, and Salome. Mark 15:40

> [50]And, behold, *there was* a man named Joseph, a counselor [council member of the Jewish council called *Sanhedrin*]; *and he was* a good man, and a just [a good and just man]: [51](The same had not consented to the counsel and deed of them [the Jews who demanded Jesus to be crucified];) *he was* of Arimathea, a city of the Jews: who also himself waited for the kingdom of God [He was a believer]. [52]This *man* went unto Pilate, and begged the body of Jesus. [53]And he took it down, and wrapped it in linen, and laid it in a sepulcher that was hewn in stone, wherein never man before was laid. Luke 23:50-53

> [38]And after this [after Jesus' death] Joseph of Arimathea, being a disciple [student, follower] of Jesus, but secretly for fear of the Jews, besought [asked] Pilate that he might take away the body of Jesus: and Pilate gave *him* leave [permission]. He came therefore, and took the body of Jesus. [39]And there came also Nicodemus, which at the first came to Jesus by night, and brought a mixture of myrrh and aloes, about a hundred pound *weight*. [40]Then took they the body of Jesus, and wound

[bound] it in linen clothes [strips] with the spices, as the manner of the Jews is to bury. [41]Now in the place where he was crucified there was a garden; and in the garden a new sepulcher [tomb], wherein was never man yet laid. [42]There laid they Jesus therefore because of the Jews' preparation *day*; for the sepulcher was nigh [nearby] at hand. John 19:38-42

For I delivered unto you first of all that which I also received, how that Christ died for our sins according to the scriptures; 1 Corinthians 15:3

For he hath made him *to be* sin for us, who knew no sin; that we might be made the righteousness of God in him. 2 Corinthians 5:21

How much more shall the blood of Christ, who through the eternal Spirit offered himself without spot [blemish] to God, purge [cleanse] your conscience from dead works to serve the living God? Hebrews 9:14

The shed blood of all those *physically* spotless animals that were sacrificed in the Old Testament could not cleanse the soul. They were only good for temporary forgiveness. But the *blood* of Christ who was without *moral* blemish—totally sinless, His death resulted in *eternal* righteousness in the eyes of God for those who accept Him.

> *Who committed no sin, Nor was deceit found in His mouth*; 1 Peter 2:22 NKJV

Isaiah 53:10: Yet it pleased the LORD [His Father] to bruise [crush] him [Jesus]; he [the Father] hath put *him* to grief: when thou shalt make his soul an offering for sin, he shall see *his* seed [He will be resurrected from the dead], he shall prolong *his* days [for all eternity], and the pleasure of the LORD shall prosper in his hand [God the Father will be satisfied with all who believe that His Son has taken their punishment and know they will also be raised from the dead because of their belief].

Isaiah 53:10 prophecy fulfilled in the New Testament:
Behold the Lamb of God, which taketh away the sin of the world. John 1:29b

Whom God hath raised up, having loosed [destroyed] the pains [birth pangs] of death: because it was not possible that he should be holden of [held by] it. Acts 2:24

But if the Spirit of him that raised up Jesus from the dead dwell in you, he that raised up Christ from the dead dwell in you, he that raised up Christ from the dead shall also quicken [give life to] your mortal bodies by [because of] his Spirit that dwelleth in you.
Romans 8:11

Isaiah 53:11: He shall see the travail [distress] of his soul, *and* shall be satisfied: by his knowledge shall my righteous servant justify many; for he shall bear their iniquities.

Isaiah 53:11 prophecy fulfilled in the New Testament:
Whom God [the Father] hath set forth *to be* a propitiation [the Father's satisfaction] through faith in His [Jesus'] blood to declare his righteousness for the remission of sins that are past, through the forbearance of God. Romans 3:25

And that he was buried, and that he rose again the third day according to the scriptures. 1 Corinthians 15:4

And God hath both raised up the Lord, and will also raise up us by his own power. 1 Corinthians 6:14

And God hath both raised up the Lord, and will also raise up us by his own power. 2 Corinthians 4:14

[13]But I would not have you to be ignorant, brethren, concerning them which are asleep [have fallen asleep, are dead], that ye sorrow not, even as others which have no hope. [14]For if we believe that Jesus died and rose again, even so them also which sleep in Jesus will God bring [to heaven] with him. [15]For this we say unto you by the word of the Lord, that we which are alive *and* remain unto [until] the coming of the Lord shall not prevent [precede] them which are asleep [dead and believed and could never stop believing]. [16]For the Lord himself shall descend from heaven with a shout, with the voice of the archangel, and with the trump [*trumpet* sounding to end the Church Age] of God: and the dead in Christ shall rise first: [17]Then we which are alive *and* remain shall be caught up together with them in the clouds, to meet the Lord in the air ["He shall see" us of whom He suffered for with "travail"—severe toil and pain]: and so shall we ever [*always*] be with the Lord. [18]Wherefore comfort one another with these words.
1 Thessalonians 4:13-18

And they [the raptured believers] sung a new song, saying, Thou art worthy to take the book [scroll], and to open the seals [each seal revealing the wrath of God to come to the unbelievers left on earth] thereof: for thou wast slain, and hast redeemed us to God by thy blood out of every kindred [tribe], and tongue, and people, and nation; Revelation 5:9

Therefore if any man *be* in Christ, *he is* a new creature: old things are passed away; behold, all things are become new. 2 Corinthians 5:17

[10]And hast made us unto our God kings and priests: and we shall reign on the earth [when we return with Him in His Second Coming at the end of the Great Tribulation]. [11]And I beheld, and I heard the voice of many angels round about the throne and the beasts [believers who become new *living creatures* (2 Cor. 5:17)] and the elders [elders of the Church Age]: and the number of them was ten thousand times ten thousand, and thousands of thousands; [12]Saying with a loud voice Worthy is the Lamb that was slain to receive power, and riches, and wisdom, and strength, and honor, and glory, and blessing. Revelation 5:10-12

Isaiah 53:12: Therefore will I divide him *a portion* with the great, and he shall divide the spoil [plunder] with the strong; because he hath poured out his soul unto death: and he was numbered with the transgressors; and he bare the sin of many, and made intercession for the transgressors.

Isaiah 53:12 prophecy fulfilled in the New Testament:
[27]And with him they crucify two thieves [robbers]; the one on his right hand, and the other on his left. [28]And the scripture was fulfilled, which saith, AND HE WAS NUMBERED WITH THE TRANSGRESSORS.
Mark 15:27-28

Fulfilled prophecies stir the heart to contemplate belief.

When the human mind discerns the written Word, then God's awesome greatness and loving kindness produce within us a love in return, and the hope we have for everlasting life.

> "But of him ye are in Christ Jesus,
> who of God is made unto us wisdom."
> 1 Corinthians 1:30a

Discernment develops reasoning ability:
> Come now, and let us reason together, saith the LORD: though your sins be as scarlet, they shall be as white as snow; though they be red like crimson, they shall be as wool. Isaiah 1:18

"The wise listen to advice" Proverbs 12:15b NIV

Endnotes

1. American Dictionary of the English Language, Noah Webster 1828, Permission to reprint granted by G. C. Merriam Company, Copyright 1967 & 1995 (Renewal) by Rosalie J. Slater. Definition of *belief* #1 and #2

2. "Election and Predestination" Authored by Peter Kerr, compiled and edited by Eunice Free, Copyright © 2020 by Everyday Publications Inc. p. 266

3. American Dictionary of the English Language, Noah Webster 1828, Permission to reprint granted by G. C. Merriam Company, Copyright 1967 & 1995 (Renewal) by Rosalie J. Slater. Definition of *discernment*

4. Ibid. Definition of verb discern

5. Ibid. Definition of doctrine #1

6. The New WEBSTER Encyclopedic DICTIONARY of the ENGLISH LANGUAGE published by CONSOLIDATED BOOK PUBLISHERS Chicago Copyright © MCMLXIX, MCMLXIX, MCMLXVIII, MCMLXVII. MCMLXV, MCMLXLXIV, MCMLII by Processing & Books, Inc. Definition of *detect*

7. Ibid. Definition of *discern*

8. American Dictionary of the English Language, Noah Webster 1828, Permission to reprint granted by G. C. Merriam Company, Copyright 1967 & 1995 (Renewal) by Rosalie J. Slater. – Definition of *solid* #6

9. Ibid. Definition of *truth* #1

10. The New Strong's Expanded Exhaustive Concordance of the Bible, © 2001 by Thomas Nelson Publishers. Hebrew and Aramaic Dictionary Section; p. 139 #3820 #1

11. American Dictionary of the English Language, Noah Webster 1828, Permission to reprint granted by G. C. Merriam Company, Copyright 1967 & 1995 (Renewal) by Rosalie J. Slater. # 8, 9

12. American Dictionary of the English Language, Noah Webster 1828, Permission to reprint granted by G. C. Merriam Company, Copyright 1967 & 1995 (Renewal) by Rosalie J. Slater. - 3rd definition of *right #1*

13. Ibid. *righteous # 1*

14. Ibid. definition of *righteous #1*

15. MATTHEW HENRY'S COMMENTARY ON THE WHOLE BIBLE, Completer and Unabridged in One Volume, Copyright@1991 by Hendrickson Publishers, Inc. Commentary on Matthew 24:4-31, p. 1738, Column 3.

16. *MIND FRAMES Where life's battle is won or lost*, Copyright ©2004, Published by Gospel Folio Press, p. 38

17. The New Strong's Expanded Exhaustive Concordance of the Bible, © 2001 by Thomas Nelson Publishers. Hebrew and Aramaic Dictionary Section:.p. 264 # 7453

18. American Dictionary of the English Language, Noah Webster 1828, Permission to reprint granted by G. C. Merriam Company, Copyright 1967 & 1995 (Renewal) by Rosalie J. Slater. #5

19. Believer's Bible Commentary, Thomas Nelson Publishers, Inc. Copyright © 1995, 1992, 1990, 1989 by William MacDonald, p. 1614, (commentary on Acts 10:44-48)

20. American Dictionary of the English Language, Noah Webster 1828, Permission to reprint granted by G. C. Merriam Company, Copyright 1967 & 1995 (Renewal) by Rosalie J. Slater, Definition of Redemption #6

21. *MIND FRAMES Where life's battle is won or lost*, Copyright ©2004, Published by Gospel Folio Press, pp. 42, 43

22. American Dictionary of the English Language, Noah Webster 1828, Permission to reprint granted by G. C. Merriam Company, Copyright 1967 & 1995 (Renewal) by Rosalie J. Slater. Definition of *education*.

23. The New Strong's Expanded Exhaustive Concordance of the Bible, © 2001 by Thomas Nelson Publishers. Hebrew and Aramaic Dictionary Section: p. 270 #7626

24. The King James Study Bible (previously published as The Liberty Annotated Study Bible and as The Annotated Study bible, King James Version) Copyright 1988 by Liberty University. Commentary on Proverbs 13:24, p. 976

25. Vine's Expository Dictionary of Old and New Testament words © 1996, Published in 1997 by Thomas Nelson, Inc., Nashville, Tennessee.

26. The New Strong's Expanded Exhaustive Concordance of the Bible, © 2001 by Thomas Nelson Publishers. Greek Dictionary of the New Testament Section: pp. 245-246 # 4991

27. The King James Study Bible (previously published as The Liberty Annotated Study Bible and as The Annotated Study bible, King James Version) Copyright 1988 by Liberty University, p. 203, commentary on "Holiness of God."

28. Ibid. p. 203

29. The King James Study Bible (previously published as The Liberty Annotated Study Bible and as The Annotated Study bible, King James Version) Copyright 1988 by Liberty University. Commentary on Leviticus 17:10-16, pp. 200-201

30. Commentary from *The King James Study Bible* (previously published as the Liberty Annotated Study Bible and as the Annotated Study Bible, King James Version) Copyright 1988 by Liberty University. Commentary on Genesis 1:1, p. 5

31. The New Strong's Expanded Exhaustive Concordance of the Bible, © 2001 by Thomas Nelson Publishers. Hebrew and Aramaic Dictionary Section: p178 and Greek Dictionary of the New Testament Section: p. 267 #7549

32. www.gotquestions.org ... How we got the Bible (20 Dec 2020)

33. MATTHEW HENRY'S COMMENTARY ON THE WHOLE BIBLE Copyright © 1991 by Hendrickson Publishers, Inc. p. 243 Chapter 5 II

34. American Dictionary of the English Language, Noah Webster 1828, Permission to reprint granted by G. C. Merriam Company, Copyright 1967 & 1995 (Renewal) by Rosalie J. Slater.

35. Believer's Bible Commentary, Thomas Nelson Publishers, Inc. Copyright © 1995, 1992, 1990, 1989 by William MacDonald, p. 2381, (commentary on Revelation 22:18, 19)

36. The King James Study Bible (previously published as The Liberty Annotated Study Bible and as The Annotated Study bible, King James Version) Copyright 1988 by Liberty University. Commentary on Romans 1:18, "Wrath of God" p. 1730

37. Ibid. "Cosmological Argument for the Existence of God" p. 1730

38. Merriam-Webster changes its definition of 'sexual preference... (14 Oct 2020) https://www.foxnews.com/politics/merriam-webster-changed-definition-sexual-preference-barrett-hearing

39. Ibid. Steve Krakauer Tweet @SteveKrak (via @ThorSvensonn & @chadfelixg) (14 Oct 2020)

40. Ibid. Article by Morgan Phillips (14 Oct 2020)

41. American Dictionary of the English Language, Noah Webster 1828, Permission to reprint granted by G. & C, Merriam Company, Copyright 1967 & 1995 (Renewal) by Rosalie J. Slater. The dictionary also simply calls fornication *Adultery.*

42. Holman Illustrated Bible Dictionary © 2003 by Holman Bible Publishers Nashville, Tennessee p. 1469

43. *Seeds of Destiny, A Genesis Devotional,* p. 10, by Warren Henderson Copyright ©2004, Published by Gospel Folio Press

44. https://weather.com/en-IN/india/news/news/2018-06-29-fish-fossil-himalayas (June 2019)

45. *The Wall Chart of World History*, Drawn by Professor Edward Hull, M.A., LLD., FRS., Copyright © Studio Editions Ltd., 1988.

46. The New Strong's Expanded Exhaustive Concordance of the Bible, © 2001 by Thomas Nelson Publishers. Hebrew and Aramaic Dictionary Section: p. 178 and Greek Dictionary of the New Testament Section: p. 176 #5030

47. American Dictionary of the English Language, Noah Webster 1828, Permission to reprint granted by G. & C, Merriam Company, Copyright 1967 & 1995 (Renewal) by Rosalie J. Slater.

48. The New Strong's, Op. cit., Greek Dictionary Section p. 216, #4396.

49. American Dictionary of the English Language. Op. cit.

50. The New WEBSTER *Encyclopedic* DICTIONARY of the ENGLISH LANGUAGE published by CONSOLIDATED BOOK PUBLISHERS Chicago Copyright © MCMLXIX, MCMLXIX, MCMLXVIII, MCMLXVII. MCMLXV, MCMLXLXIV, MCMLII by Processing & Books, Inc., Definition of *prophecy; prophesy* within description.

51. *Forsaken, Forgotten and Forgiven—A Devotional Study of Jeremiah and Lamentations* (second edition) By Warren Henderson Copyright © 2016 p. 330

52. The Atlantic 20 July 2021, https://www.theatlantic.com > tomb-of-jonah-mosul-isis

53. F. B. Meyer, *Christ in Isaiah* p. 126

54. American Dictionary of the English Language, Noah Webster 1828, Permission to reprint granted by G. C. Merriam Company, Copyright 1967 & 1995 (Renewal) by Rosalie J. Slater. Definition of truth #1, third sentence

55. *Infidelity and Loyalty—A Devotional Study of Ezekiel and Daniel* By Warren Henderson Copyright © 2017 pp 392-393

About the Author

Michael Copple's life experience includes twenty-six years active duty in the US Air Force, nine years of which were overseas, including one year in Vietnam, and nine years with the Wings of Blue Parachute Team at the U.S. Air Force Academy. From 1983 to 1986, he was the Superintendent of Parachuting Operations at USAF Academy. He has logged over 2,000 parachute jumps with fifteen hours of freefall, and he earned jump wings from six foreign countries. Michael obtained the highest enlisted rank of Chief Master Sergeant.

He holds a BS degree in electrical engineering. And after retiring from the Air Force, he worked for a semiconductor tool and robotics manufacturing company as service engineer, trainer, and technical writer.

He survived several near-death events including four parachute malfunctions, a night equipment jump entanglement with another jumper, being hung up to the outside of an aircraft at 3,000 feet above ground level, and he was caught in an 85mph wind shear under canopy—and more. You can read all about his parachute malfunctions and what it feels like in his novel "Calling from the Sky".

Michael realized that his God-given purpose is to devote his time to authoring Christian literature and bringing forth God's Word.

This has now been his goal for the past 16 years.

Michael Copple, a permanent resident of Canada since 2003, has resided near Golden, B.C., with his Canadian wife, Elfriede. They both believe that the Lord Jesus Christ is indeed the Son of God, enjoy reading and studying God's Word, cross country skiing, hiking, and walking every day with their dog "Kansas".

Visit Michael and read more about him on his website/blog at: https://michaelcopple.com/

Books by Michael Copple

Considering Wisdom
Gold or Wisdom - What will it be?
    ISBN: 978-1-9736-9622-3 (sc)
    ISBN: 978-1-9736-9623-0 (hc)
    ISBN: 978-1-9736-9621-6 (e)

Digging Deep into The Revelation of Jesus Christ
A Study Guide - Second Edition

    ISBN: 978-1-9736-4917-5 (sc)
    ISBN: 978-1-9736-4916-8 (e)

    Exam Booklet to the Study Guide
    ISBN: 978-1-7778325-1-3 (sc)
    ISBN: 978-1-7778325-0-6 (e)

Calling from the Sky
A Novel Inspired by True Events
    ISBN: 978-1-9736-6903-6 (sc)
    ISBN: 978-1-9736-6904-3 (hc)
    ISBN: 978-1-9736-6902-9 (e)

CPSIA information can be obtained
at www.ICGtesting.com
Printed in the USA
LVHW071924180322
713807LV00001B/1